SHETLAND

Land of the Ocean

First published in Great Britain in 1992 by

Colin Baxter Photography Ltd
Grantown-on-Spey, Moray,
Scotland, PH26 3NA

First published in paperback in 1995
Reprinted 1998

Photographs © Colin Baxter 1992
Text © Jim Crumley 1992
All Rights Reserved

A CIP catalogue record for this book is available from the British Library
ISBN I 900455 94 3

Black & White Illustrations © Darroch Donald
Map by Oxford Illustrators Ltd

Front cover photograph
Gaada Stack, Foula.

Back cover photograph
Eshaness, North Mainland.

Printed in Hong Kong

SHETLAND

Land of the Ocean

Colin Baxter and Jim Crumley

Colin Baxter Photography Ltd, Grantown-on-Spey, Scotland

SHETLAND – LAND OF THE OCEAN

Map

Introduction

Bibliography

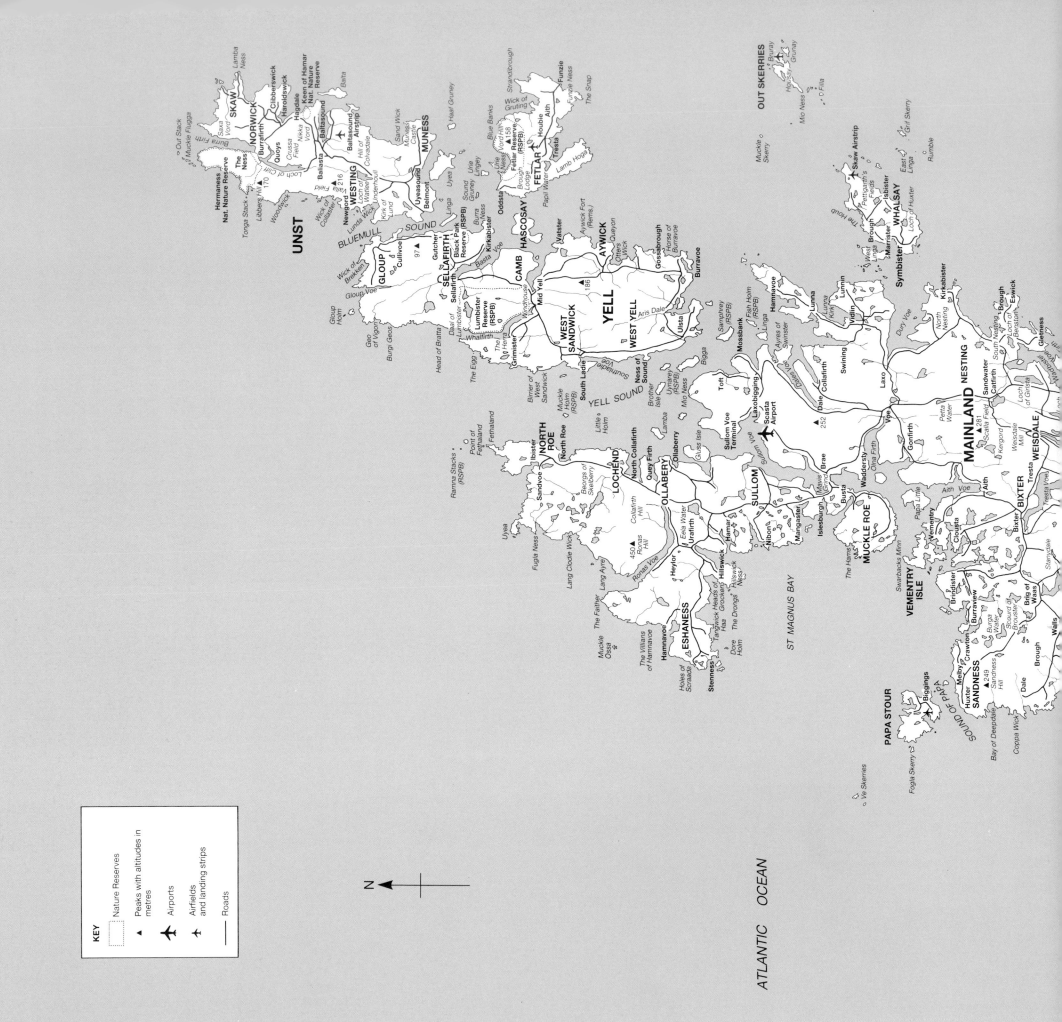

SKAW
NORWICK
Lamba Ness
Burrafirth
Clibberswick
Haroldswick
Keen of Hamar
Nat. Nature Reserve
Hagdale
Saxa Vord
Nikka Vord
Balta
Baltasound
Airstrip
UNST
Out Stack
Muckle Flugga
Hermaness
Nat. Nature Reserve
The Ness
170
Loch of Cliff
Crussa Field
Hill of Colvadale
Muness Castle
MUNESS
Tonga Stack
Libbers Hill
Ballasta
Valla Field 216
Sand Wick
Woodwick
WESTING
Newgord
Underhoull
Loch of Watlee
Uyea
Haaf Gruney
Wick of Breikken
Kirk of Lund
Lunda Wick
Wick of Collaster
Uyeasound
Belmont
Linga
Uyea
Sound Gruney
Uie Lingey
Uie Ness
Blue Banks
Wick of Gruting
Strandibrough
GLOUP
Cullivoe
97
Gutcher
Gloup Holm
Gloup Voe
BLUEMULL
SOUND
Sellafirth
SELLAFIRTH
Basta
Kirkabister
Burra Voe
Vatster
CAMB
Mid Yell
Uyea
Houll 158
Oddsta
Brough
Papil Water
FETLAR
Fetlar Nature Reserve (RSPB)
Funzie
Aith
Houbie
Tresta
Funzie Ness
The Snap
Lamb Hoga
OUT SKERRIES
Bruray
Housay
Grunay
Mio Ness
D Filla
Geo of Vigon
Burgi Geos
Head of Bratta
Deal of Lumbister
Lumbister Reserve (RSPB)
The Herra
The Eigg
Grimister
Whalfirth
WEST SANDWICK
Windhouse
YELL
186
Aris Dale
WEST YELL
Ulsta
AYWICK
Otters Wick
Aywick Fort (Rems.)
Queyon
Gossabrough
Horse of Burravoe
Burravoe
Skaw Airstrip
Pettigarth's Fields
WHALSAY
Isbister
Marrister
Symbister
Kirkabister
Loch of Huxter
The Houb
West Linga
East Linga
Muckle Skerry
Girt Skerry
Rumble
Birrier of West Sandwick
Muckle Holm (RSPB)
Little Holm
Southlade
South Ladie
Ness of Sound
Brother Isle
Uynarey (RSPB)
Mio Ness
Gluss Isle
Lamba
Bigga
Samphrey
YELL SOUND
Mossbank
Fish Holm
Hamnavoe
Lunna
Lunna Ness
Lunna Kirk
Swining
Laxo
Vidlin
Lumbin
Dury Voe
North Nesting
Loch of Girlsta
Gletness
Ramna Stacks (RSPB)
Point of Fethaland
Fethaland
Ibister
NORTH ROE
North Roe
North Collafirth
Quey Firth
Collafirth
Sandvoe
Uyea
Collafirth Hill
450
Ronas Hill
Ronas Voe
Heylor
Eela Water
Urafirth
LOCHEND
OLLABERRY
Ollaberry
Collafirth
Gonfirth
Dale
Collafirth
252
North Nesting
MAINLAND
NESTING
Sandwater
South Nesting
Brough
Catfirth
Eswick
Scalla Field
Kergord
Weisdale Mill
WEISDALE
Tresta
Uyea
Fugla Ness
Lang Clodie Wick
Lang Ayre
The Faither
Muckle Ossa
The Villians of Hannavoe
Hammavoe
ESHANESS
Stenness
Holes of Scraada
Tangwick Heads of Grocken
Haa
Hillswick Ness
Hillswick
The Drongs
Dore Holm
Hamar
Nibon
Mangaster
Busta
Brae
Aith Voe
Aith
Papa Little
Vementry
Clousta
Brindister
BIXTER
Bixter
Tresta
Mavis Grind
Sullom Voe
SULLOM
Islesburgh
Wadtersty
Olna Firth
Voe
MUCKLE ROE
The Hams
Swarbacks Minn
VEMENTRY ISLE
Burga Water
Stroud of Brouster
Burraview
Stanydale
SANDNESS
Huxter
Melby
Crawton
249
Sandness Hill
Dale
Walls
Brough
Brig of Waas
Bay of Deepdale
Coppa Wick
Sullom Voe Terminal
Toft
Laxobigging
Laxo
Scatsta Airport
Scatsta Airport
Ayres of Swinister
Linga
Petta Water
WESTING
ST MAGNUS BAY
PAPA STOUR
Biggings
Ve Skerries
Fogla Skerry
SOUND OF PAPA

KEY

Nature Reserves

Peaks with altitudes in metres

Airports

Airfields and landing strips

Roads

N

ATLANTIC OCEAN

INTRODUCTION

SHETLAND IS a place which responds well to a seeing eye and a listening ear. I have always inclined to the idea that the way to learn about a new place is to watch and listen to the landscape, remarking how people and nature (an indivisible duology here) pass over it, how they shape it and how they are shaped by it. I believe, too, that it is no bad thing to pack something of a poet's instinct when you travel to watch a landscape, for it sharpens the eye and hones the hearing. Such an eye and ear and instinct will never struggle for sustenance in this Shetland of oceanic landscapes.

But first, a brief human story should be told. That story is well and famously documented, and many of the uncountable volumes in the Shetland Room in Lerwick's public library, pore over it, dissect it, argue about it with varying degrees of expertise and authority. The truth in all its bloody detail is doubtless there somewhere, but not the whole truth, for there are many blank chapters in Shetland's story. So this brief introductory account is a skeleton of a skeleton, a historical platform from which the poet has launched and voyaged. It helped me, it may help you.

It is no pilgrimage of saints you follow when you set sail from Scotland to Shetland. Villainy has preceded you, and centuries of sustained villainy at that. The characteristic seafaring adventurousness of Scots has won them friends in many corners of the world. Shetland is not one of them. If you are new to Shetland, you may perceive a contradiction here. Surely Shetland *is* Scottish? To be sure, the islands were annexed by the Scottish Crown in 1469, but despite the subsequent corruption and criminal hedonism of the next 400 years or so, Shetland remains about as Scottish as the Isle of Wight, which is more or less equidistant from Edinburgh too. Today, of course, Shetland is nominally British, which makes even less sense, for it lies 1,000 miles from London, but only 200 from the Norwegian coast. One way or another, Shetland has always suffered from being where it is. One way or another, it still does and always will.

Shetland is a gathering of more or less 100 islands, depending on how you define 'island', and where you draw the line between an island and a rock, a skerry, and other diminutives. More or less a quarter are still inhabited, but it is a long time since that figure did anything but dwindle and it dwindles still. The landscape has done much the same thing, for over the millennia, the mountains which once stood where Shetland now lies have shrivelled to molehills, and the sea has risen. Orkney was cut adrift from Caithness 13,000 years ago, by which time Shetland was already an archipelago. But man did not infiltrate the islands until the 4th century BC, and even then he showed a marked preference for the fertile, low-slung Orkney. Navigating within the limits of good visibility, it would take two quantum leaps of daring to push north to Fair Isle and then to Shetland, for Fair Isle is the one visible stepping stone between the two island realms, 25 miles or so from both of them, but don't let the Fair Isle folk catch you calling their island a stepping stone.

It is tempting to think of such people as those first settlers as primitives. The monuments of their passing suggest otherwise. They were organised, they had sophisticated minds, and they imported rich rituals and traditions. They came exclusively from the south, navigating Europe's western seaboard, their spoor betrayed by similar evidence in Caithness, for example. There was no infiltration from the east, not yet.

The land has changed since their time. Their slow growth in population would account for the slow demise of such tree cover as there was, many sparse and small woodlands. Shetland was never thickly wooded, and never even as wooded as Orkney once was, but the mysterious broch builders could well have known woods of birch and willow and hazel in the sheltered valleys, as recently as 1,000 BC. But with the decline of the trees, the worsening of the climate (colder, windier), the spread of hill and moor grasses, the thickening of peat, the insidious advance of sheep (and what are euphemistically known as the 'Highland' Clearances happened here too), the land evolved a harsher character. It is still harsh, harsh but inimitably beautiful.

It was a Pictish realm which Christian missionaries found sometime after the Romans came and saw and declined to conquer, keeping a respectful distance and heeling south again, and it was a Pictish civilisation which held fast until the one great invasion from which Shetland never recovered, and from which even today, it shows no great wish to recover, the conquest around 800 AD by the Vikings.

The Vikings raided far more than Shetland, of course, and their influence was felt to one extent or another far up and down the shores of mainland Scotland and England, and among all their islands. But in Shetland, and to only a marginally lesser extent in Orkney, the cultural conversion was permanent and its spirit clings still. The islands were administered from Norway until a callous wedding arrangement between James III of Scotland and Christian I of Norway and Denmark transferred them almost nonchalantly to the Scottish Crown, and that was that. The deal was that as part of the dowry for James' bride Margaret, the islands of Orkney and Shetland would be annexed to Scotland, but redeemable on payment of 50,000 florins. At first only Orkney was annexed, but when the impoverished Norwegians failed to make good the pledge, Shetland was acquired for a further 8,000 florins, and there are those in today's Orkney who will put their tongues in their cheeks and tell you that's about right. Shetland has suffered many grievous fates in its time and many outrages, but it has only been horse-traded once.

During James V's visit to Kirkwall in 1540 a sheriff of Orkney and Shetland was appointed, after which the rot really set in, and a vile and relentless process of compulsory Scottification began. Scotland has good cause to protest over the centuries at many forms of inflicted Anglicisation, but the history of Shetland from 1540 until embarrassingly recently is one of unflattering exploitation by a certain class of obnoxious Scots. As the *Inventory of Historical Monuments for Orkney and Shetland* put it in 1946:

'But the beginning of the new regime was memorable for a great deal more than the growth of Scottish influence, as in 1567 began the last and longest period of misgovernment that the Islands have been called to suffer at the hands of Scottish adventurers.'

Three years before, Mary Queen of Scots had set the misgovernment in motion by giving the Crown estates of Orkney and Shetland to her half brother Robert Stewart, who used his position and his power and his corrupt nature to milk the islands dry. He raised rents, took land when it suited him, interfered in trade and made a farce of the law by manipulating the courts at his whim. It was clearly a family failing for his son's reign was even more corrupt and self-centred, and included forced labour (by which Scalloway Castle was built), initiated a licence system to sell anything at all - and guess who sold the licences - and quite usurped the legislative powers. Even when he had gone so far over the score that a bishop's complaint to the King resulted in his arrest, he egged on his own son, and that wretch's five-week siege of Kirkwall ended in farce. Eventually, they were both executed.

By this time, of course, the islands had become British, and much good it did them, apart from the fact that in 1643, Charles II built Fort Charlotte above the Sound of Bressay and inadvertently gave birth to Lerwick in the process. There followed 200 years or so of sundry sallies north by favourites of the royal court in Scotland, lairds who built fine houses and carved up the islands into estates, and subjected the islanders to yet more humiliations as a race of little more than feudal underlings.

The Scots language travelled with these unwelcome intruders and forced the islanders to become reluctantly bilingual. One historian noted that 'at the end of the 17th century the language of the people of south Dunrossness was Scots, though all could speak the Gothick or Norwegian tongue, while in the north of the parish, though Scots was spoken, the people seldom used anything but Gothick among themselves'.

By the mid-18th century only Foula clung to the pure Shetland dialect of Norn. Lowland Scots slowly withered it away throughout the other islands. But even today there is a distinctly Norse cadence to what has become Shetland English (for Scots, too, has withered almost to extinction), and a smattering of a 'Shetlandic' vocabulary survives.

So if you voyage north to Shetland today (and if you are a Scot it is as well not to assume you are travelling to an outpost of your native land), go with your eyes and ears open and marvel. For all that has been lost here, there are still glimpses and hints of that northern ancestry, still wildlife riches - especially birds - in thrilling numbers, still, best of all, the mesmerism of the land itself and the seas which infuse its every waking, sleeping, breathing, breathless moment. It may be no pilgrimage of saints you follow, but you will find the pilgrimage in what is a kindlier era for Shetland no less worthwhile for that.

Chapter One

THE LAND OF THE SWORD

THE CLUTCHER at history's straws considers the word 'Shetland'. He draws a not completely fanciful conclusion that the last 1,000 years of all its variations, including 'Hetland' and 'Hjaltland', derive from the Norse 'hjalt', rhe crosspiece of a sword. The poet hefts the definition to see how it feels, brandishes it with some satisfaction. Look at the map. Grasp the headlands of Delting in your hand. Finger the crosspiece from Sandness to Whalsay (from Papa Stour to Out Skerries if you like your hjalt well garnished). See the blade glitter dully down to Sumburgh Head, a steely sheen of rain on wet rock. Northmaven, if you must, can be your basket hilt. The landscape also fits the definition well, for it depends for its effect on a coalition of its extremities, its sea-cutting edges, the discreet strength of its bladed rock, the brown scabbard of peat-deep hills.

It is more a definition for poets than scholars, perhaps, but what poet worth the title would settle for the preferred academic option that the name is a corruption of some ancient and lost relic? A pre-Norse hint which moulders darkly? A second Jarlshof, entombed in peat? It intrigues the poet, of course, but only slightly, because it is too easy, too unsatisfactory, too comfortably inconclusive, so he wields his Sword-land again and finds it a good and fitting symbol for these most sword-smitten of islands.

Now, however, he fences with a dilemma, for the symbolic sword to which he has thirled his instincts is only the middle of Shetland, that portion of its island flock which the more - but rarely the Shetlanders - call Mainland, and its immediate seagoing outriders. Beyond, another ferry or two away, another anguished hour or two for the oarsmen of coracle and longship, lie the North Sea islands, the Atlantic islands, the fragment islands off every shore, the lap-of-the-gods islands of Foula and Fair Isle. Even within the baffled isolation which Britain confers on Shetland by casting it adrift somewhere off Aberdeen like a discarded fishbox, there are degrees of isolation, furthest-flung corners of this furthest-flung corner. These seem to take no part in the poet's swordplay, so what of them? He prowls their sea-riven midst, unearths the best of Shetland here, the sharpest Shetland savour, the truest adherence to the island nature of that Shetland which was written Hjaltland. It is possible on today's Shetland Mainland - say in Brae in a March haar - to forget the island rootedness of where you stand. It is never possible on Fetlar or Noss or Foula. The outlier islands, the poet concludes, are the jewelled regalia of Shetland, secure in the strong room of the seas. The sword at the heart of the island flock is their symbolic strength, in the way that a sword of Wallace once united diffuse Scots, just as the scattering of the flock is its own true strength. Independence is underpinned by interdependence, individuality is shackled lightly and loyally to the common tribal bond, and the sea is its ultimate unity. Every island lies in the lee of all the others as Shetland's virtuosic repertoire of winds bedevils every compass point.

So the poet finds his instincts well served by his Sword-land preference, or perhaps he has merely made his vision of the islands fit his cause, for that is any poet's privilege. It is an appropriate enough privilege too, for the Viking sagas which fed so eagerly off Shetland are the work of poets with battleaxes to grind, not fact-finders. The academic when he is defeated, can pass on to the next conundrum, cheerfully unfulfilled, his every shred of evidence exhausted. The poet cannot. He lingers restlessly because his evidence is inexhaustible, and day after Shetland day, year after year, he must mine new artefacts from the same rich seams of light and time, landscape and tide, his sword serving his pen.

George Mackay Brown is unsurpassed as such a poet, rooted in neighbouring Orkney. This is his own job-description, a poem called 'The Poet':

> Therefore he no more troubled the pool of silence
> But put on mask and cloak,
> Strung a guitar
> And moved among the folk.
> Dancing they cried,
> 'Ah, how our sober islands
> Are gay again, since this blind lyrical tramp
> Invaded the Fair!'
>
> Under the last dead lamp
> When all the dancers and masks had gone inside
> His cold stare
> Returned to its true task, interrogation of silence.

I sail with the poet in all this. I find in these bright and quicksilvery lights, these charging winds and wide skies, these curved and cut island profiles and all their permeating seas, a day-long swordplay of mesmerising agility.

That illusion of agility is further fuelled by a four-season swirl of birds. There came, for example, a day of spring-less May (the hills still wintry brown, the Sound of Bressay the moody preserve of swaabies, bonxies and tysties (great black-backed gulls, great skuas and black guillemots hereabouts) when a single Arctic tern - tirrick in the same percussive island tongue - alighted on top of the mast of Lerwick harbour's Viking galley just above its blue and white Shetland flag. Now there's a foregathering of symbolism for you! The tern, addictive sea cruiser, enslaved to the colonising of perpetually foreign shores, then spurring nomadically north and south in season; the longship, symbol of the Vikings' tirrick instincts to which Shetland still pays homage more than 500 years after irresistible south winds of change compelled the Norsemen to one last northerly flight.

The tern, though, was also a harbinger. The next day, there were a dozen out west by Vementry, the next there were thousands billeted on all Shetland's watersheets - voe, loch, lochan, pond - and the islands grew loud with their shouts, drifted deep in their bird snow. They whispered down on sand eels in Nibon's South Sound, and screeched up into the chaotic flock, giving and receiving ritual chase, quibbling or posturing, proposing and repelling, marshalling flimsily vicious forces to thwart piratical bonxies, skipping down to tease surfacing seals. The shaldurs - oystercatchers - raged at all of that, for the female had been sitting on three stony eggs for a week, a fraught enough penance with the bonxies and the big gulls and the opportunist otters without the infuriating arrival of the terns. Her mate tore into the flock, and the air was slashed with the black-and-white-and-scarlet of all that clamorous strife.

The terns blossomed overnight, thick as flag irises, on a roadside pond on Yell. That morning warmed to the spring commitment of the birds. A pair sunned themselves determinedly in the middle of the road, and there they remained unchallenged for fully 30 minutes until Yell's midday rush hour - a limping Transit and a Reliant three-wheeler - persuaded them into reluctant flight. One day on Muckle Roe was deathly winter-still, the next a dervish horde thrummed on the loch beyond the window sill, roused tranquil households into screaming dawns. It is with the coming of the tirricks that Shetland cheers the death of winter.

For a few days more, the birds hold centrestage (the moorland and sea cliff hordes, the autumnal deluge of geese and whooper swans and waders all have their hour of glory, an ambassadorial welcome), then Shetland's landscape truth reasserts itself. It is that the bird tides' ebb and flow are simply one more shifting component of the perpetually shifting landscape, heightening the illusion of agility. The land itself flickers beyond the terns, dazzles beyond the whoopers, clouds massively gray beyond the raining geese, harlequins gaily above and below the tammy nories, which is Shetland for puffins. Each new bird spectacle is quickly absorbed into the landscape mix. The eyes adjust, tone it down, search out the next advance down the sea wind.

Birds and islands and ocean winds conspire in unlimited adventures, flocks of plots fashioned by the most bizarre of scripts. Some reverberate through the country in newsreels and bold headlines, like Fetlar's superstar snowy owls and Hermaness's lonely black-browed albatross, luring fast migrations of bird-watching twitchers to the oblivious midst of the birds' fortunes or misfortunes. Some darken the sky in fleeting thousands, even hundreds of thousands. Some make furtive solitary voyages which overwhelm oceans with tiny determination and the ornithological records of Shetland are wonder-filled with their like.

The most cynically worked scripts of all these plots of winged endeavour are surely those which direct this storm or that to bring its Shetland voyaging to bear on the sporadic vagrancy of a tree creeper. Imagine the turmoil within such a frail and storm-stupefied bird spying the far landfall of Shetland and finding there no loose-barked leafy havens but an archipelago of treeless deserts. Do such birds home in on oases - the meagre plantations of Kergord or the gardens of Busta House - or do they mope south snatching hungrily at the unpalatable salt fare of shingles as they go, surviving only if they chance on Orkney's flimsy woods or the startling green plaid which wraps Tongue on Sutherland's far north coast? Either way, it is an ill-wind which propels such tree-thirled birds to Shetland, but it is just one small play in the game of islands and ocean winds in which the flung birds curse or bless their landfall.

The wind permits no lethargies of the soul for the Shetlander. His relationship with the wind is like the land's with the sea, a well-wedded conflict which varies only in the degrees of its withering assault. The land is compelled to stand up to the sea, for cowardice is not an option in the warring of the elements, and just as forcibly compelled to comply with its sacrificial demands - a limb, a headland, a beach. The Shetlander's life is also a courageous compliance which bows to the overlordship of the winds. He leans stoically into their relentlessness while the land leans into the sea's advance, patient for executions. At their dark, winter worst, the winds are a wearisome dirge; at their high-skied spring-bright best, they eddy the land in songs. The Shetlander has long since learned to mourn and sing with the wind's moods, long since learned to adjust his step and his stance, the shrug of his shoulders and the set of his sail to his winds. The incomer or the fly-by-night rarely learns to master the psychology of the wind's demands, and can often be quite defeated by them.

The landscape of today's Shetland is moulded by another feather-ruffling air, a wind of change, which like all Shetland's prevailing winds, leaves an indelible signature. Shetland's whole story is written by such traumatic winds, each with a capacity to flatten and trample the past determinedly underfoot. Few, if any, have signed themselves so ruthlessly as this last wind. It blows in many guises, this ill-at-ease wind, and a sense of the change it bears is stamped even on the very thresholds of all Shetland.

It erupts along Lerwick's waterfronts where the old is a huddled beguilement of comforting stone knee deep in the sea. The new, thoughtless, unplanned, impersonal, keeps its distance from the sea because it does not know how to build there and cannot take the time to learn. One is built on rock, in the great tradition of sea places throughout the land, the other on the shifting sands of the oil industry. One has given Shetland the character to which the Shetlanders themselves still adhere, the other the wherewithal to buy a stake in their own independence and spare them at least some of the social rot which has set in and so bedevilled other isolated island communities. It is a paradox you dice with many times in any exploration of what Shetland has become.

A house in old Lerwick is called 'The Sea Door'. A neighbour's lock-up has an upturned boat for a roof (a traditional adaptation which lingers on in other parts of Shetland, notably on Yell). They have the Sound of Bressay for a garden, the crooning of dunters – eiders – to soothe sleep and the yelping of swaabies for an early morning alarm. Alleyways end where the seas begin. That much is as it was. Lerwick inevitably has grown from that old hub. It is the nature of its growth which dismays for it discards distinctive Shetlandness for indistinction, tradition for architectural trash.

Sumburgh is Shetland's other threshold for the world to cross, and there the wind of change wreaks its most contemptuous havocs. For there, where Shetland's throbbing airport drapes helicopters on the air like terns over a shoal of sand eels, and where all manner of prying steel sculptures scowl down from every other hilltop, lies the one phenomenon of Shetland's past more worthy and more demanding of quiet contemplation and marvelling than any other – Jarlshof.

Sir Walter Scott stitched the name onto a 16th-century house for his novel, *The Pirate*, not knowing that its laird's house ruin was the tip of a gray iceberg which reached down under the peat for 3,500 years. Your mind reels in the midst of the evidence of these tiered civilisations and at the nature of their hoarded secrets betrayed only by 20th-century storms, uncovered with increasing incredulity and wonder by 20th-century archaeologists and social and architectural historians. Yet not even the revealed presence of Jarlshof has persuaded Shetland's new winds to contemplate discretionary changes of direction.

The wide-eyed ghosts of Jarlshof doubtless foregather in the garbs of all their eras to bemoan in all their civilisations' tongues the shuddering presences which so dishevel their long sleep. 'Are our lives', they ask, 'of so little avail?'

They melt darkly down again in fear of such winds. Their dismay will find bonded sympathies in many hearts which beat in Shetland now.

I walked out late in a May evening, a quiet, graying hour among the hilltop cairns and winds of Vementry, swaabies stacked above my head like bombers, when a mountain hare sprang from under my feet, cut away across a mile of heather, paused every few hundred yards to sit cock-eared and listen, testing the wind, suspecting pursuit. She was in that transitory mottled phase of whites and browns and in-betweens which presage all the mountain hare's summers. The starkest contrast in that hare that night as she sat and stared and ran on, and wondered perhaps at the nature of my presence on her ground, was that although her back was completely brown, her ears were still unblemished white, a legacy of that winter landscape which will always be the one I hold closest. The white hare is the true hare. I imbued her then with the spirit of all Shetland, her mottled garb with the plight of Shetland's landscape in its wind of change. The brown is an inevitable phase for the hare, just as change is an inevitable fate for the garb of the Shetland which was. But I think that like the hare, it yearns in its heart of hearts to return to its winter garb, the true white of the north; I think that like the hare, Shetland still listens with white ears.

The first-time voyager to Shetland faces one unexpected obstacle as he tries to come to terms with his surroundings. He will probably use a map, and map makers have trouble with Shetland. Where on earth is it? Almost invariably it is in a box, usually in the North Sea, but these are nomadic islands and they have been known to berth alongside Orkney to the east, north-west of Orkney, and in the Solway Firth, jostling the doubtless startled inhabitants of the Isle of Man. In Shetland, you can buy a souvenir tea towel showing a map of Shetland with a little map of Britain in a box in the corner, a particularly pointed form of revenge.

Ah, but if only it were as simple as that. Here is the Official Tourist Map for 'Shetland and Orkney Islands', and there is the logo on the cover showing both groups of islands in correct position and in proportion with the north coast of Scotland below, but there is no sign of Fair Isle or Foula. There is the back cover of the same map and under the words 'Shetland and Orkney Islands' there is a map of Scotland minus Orkney and Shetland. The map is made in Kent, which may explain something, but you suspect it doesn't happen to the Isle of Wight. It does not get any better when the maps consider Shetland in close up. Here is the OS Map of 'Shetland South Mainland' and there, neatly boxed off West Burra and Fitful Head are Fair Isle and Foula. Here is a book called *The Shetland Story*: the cover is the old familiar Shetland silhouette – minus Fair Isle and Foula. Inside is a map of 'Shetland Islands' with Foula in place, but Fair Isle boxed east of Sumburgh. Here is a British Telecom leaflet with useful telephone numbers in the north of Scotland and the islands. You help yourself to them from a box at Foula's tiny airstrip, and discover that every copy has had the word 'Foula' inked in by hand, and a small dot indicating its position. But the map makers put Shetland north-west of Orkney, so that the inked-in Foula they forgot is now due north of Cape Wrath. It's bad enough being a Shetlander and trying to explain to a stranger where to find you. If you're on Fair Isle or Foula, though, you know the one thing you dare not do is send them a map.

Seasons in Shetland are just as unreliable as maps, and it can be a dislocating experience to step on a plane in the burgeoning spring of April in London or Edinburgh, and step off in a Shetland locked in the death throes of winter, daffodils clenched tight, snow on the hills, ice on the wind, no shade of green on the crofts, the land as moorit as the sheep. But persevere with it, for there will dawn a day which wakes you with its silence. The wind has finally blown itself breathless. Voes still and sparkle, and Shetlanders fall in love again with that land and those landscapes of the sea which they cursed all winter darkness long. On such a day, a blissful daze envelops the islands, and the peat reek rises straight as a longship mast. Winter is not finished with the place, of course, and there will be a few final tantrums deep into May, but the seed of spring's optimism is sown, and its blossoming only a matter of time now.

Chapter Two

THE LAND OF THE OUTER SHORE

SAND VOE hacks an axe head deep into the north coast of Northmaven (images of weaponry are irresistible, it seems, but it is a very good axe-head shape). It offers a tranquil refuge which stymies all winds but one: when a north-westerly crams fearfully through the narrows of the voe, animating air and water with awesome vigour, the wielded axe chops heartlessly at the land. Such blood-letting of the landscape is Shetland's oldest ritual, and on this crippled north coast are its most ancient survivors, for out towards the island of Uyea are Shetland's oldest rocks. It is a fit pilgrimage by way of an introduction to the land of the outer shore, both for the nature of its destination and for the characteristic elements of all Shetland's seaward edges which you encounter on the way - voes, stacks, cliffs, headlands, islands, skerries, caves, arches, gloups and geos - and all their boisterous sea birds and sea beasts, rock-happy flowers and brimming-over moorland birdsong (for all Shetland's elements are enthusiastic and mutual trespassers).

A bay unwraps beyond the voe's first headland, and you are introduced at once to four of Shetland's seagoing tribes - the skarfs, tysties, dunters and raingeese. Shetland's indigenous vocabulary is a withering blossom, much deflowered by the dead hand of English, but it clings with some fondness to its expressive repertoire of bird names. You finger these as you walk, taste them on your tongue to see how they match up to the reality of the bird you know. Skarf and tystie sit happily enough on shag and black guillemot, but dunter seems a bit brutal at first hearing for creamy-crooner eider ducks, certainly a bit drab for the drake. Raingoose is the red-throated diver, a bird I have long held in the highest esteem for the landscape company it keeps (I remember a high loch on Raasay, a higher hill lochan in the Mamores, secret places in Sutherland and Skye). Shetland is the bird's breeding stronghold, however, which is as high a recommendation of the Shetland landscape as I can offer. The 'raingoose' bit derives from the bird's legendary predilection for prophesying rain, hardly an uncanny skill given its chosen habitat. In Shetland, it mutters 'mair weet, waur wedder' as it croaks past, while in Gaeldom, where the same legend persists, it is the bird's watersheet wail which is the bad weather prophecy. Science, of course, as science will, has found more reliable explanations for the copious rainfall of Shetland and the Hebrides, better explanations for the bird's voices. It seems a pity, and wholly unnecessary, this pooh-poohing of diver lore, for when it comes to raingeese and Shetland and prophecies of rain, sooner rather than later they all come true.

So the bay boasted nine dunters and a pair of raingeese and their dalliances were gatecrashed in turn by the skarf and a tystie. The gatecrashers subsided on the water 100 feet below me, the tystie bow-waving energetically forward while scarlet paddles threshed at the stern like a Mississippi steamer, the skarf flipping up and forward and down through a full-bodied dive in pursuit of its own eel-questing nose. I watched it darken down, and in the watching, began to re-appraise the bay. It is not a bay at all but an underwater corrie. It owns not a beach but a headwall with a ledge at sea-level. The land, when it reaches the sea, dives on down and down, its verticals unimpaired, except where the sea has fathomed frailties in the underwater rock and smashed through the outer shell to feast within, like a shaldur on a mussel.

The eider flock disperses, four drakes in optimistic chase behind a single female into the now hidden sanctuary of the voe's axe head, the others - two pairs - step ashore simply to sit. The raingeese cry, a thin, grating, neck-tingling woodwind note which falls as it fades and carries effortlessly across a mile of water. They inscribe their circles on the surface, swim out and out until their low profiles are lower than the waves, until their voices drag away seaward where their prophecies will fall on the ears of a lone lobster fisherman. From the look of the northern sky, 'mair weet, waur wedder' will be about right. It usually is.

My westering tracks towards Uyea dip and dive and clamber and climb round and down and up and over bay after bay, headland after headland. A gray seal bananas on a rock, head and tail high, wearing that torpid mask her tribe reserves for that portion of life when the tide has fallen away from them and they offer the illusion at least that the effort of pursuing it is a draining of energy too hellish to contemplate. The seal in question occupies a small rock podium one seal wide, half a seal long, and with the sea on all sides, so that she lies tide-stranded 15 feet above the sea. But she is alert to my silhouette along her skyline, glissades down the rock (an unlikely gymnast) and eases something like 300 pounds splashlessly into the tide. It is a shallower dive than the skarf's, its purpose not that of the hunter but the watcher, to exercise vigilance from the sea's stronghold, to resurface with all haste, to inspect and assess the intruder. So she corks back to the surface and 'stands' her neck deep in the water, her body vertically beneath her, and her eyes watchful, for does she not dwell in that precarious limbo in which the figure on the shore might just as easily turn on her with club or gun or (should she step seductively ashore as a selkie) fall in love with the sight of her and be seduced into the troubled seas of legend? But alas for legend, all we did was watch each other a while, then we went our ways in our true elements. Beyond her, the rocks of the shore darkened away west towards Uyea, a bitten shore, the first fractured sight of Shetland's very foundation stone, perhaps 3,000 million years old.

It is an incomprehensible statistic. You feel, perhaps, you should approach such fragmentary symbolism of the millenia with an awed reverence, that there should be a wondrous presence, perhaps a sense of a geological Eden from which all Shetland flowed and scattered and heaped up and collapsed into the rocky time warps which shaped what we know as the map of Shetland. There is, of course, no such presence. Not even the tourist map's bold red lettering proclaiming 'Oldest rocks in Shetland' (as though any hewn fragment might have 'Shetland' in red all the way through it) can impart any sense of a happening. You could say that the rocks don't show their age, but how does anything show age like that? What should 3,000 million years look like?

What you do get is a sense of weariness from butting the sea back and back, a losing combatant in the oldest war in the world. There were mountains here once. Now there are headstones to mark their passing.

All along the shore now, as far as the island of Uyea which marks the top left-hand corner of all Shetland, there are caves and geos and blowholes and stacks. Once you have arranged in your eye some sense of order amid that dark shambles, they resemble nothing so much as a collapsed railway tunnel. The seaward light throws an impenetrable blackness on the westward rocks, a tawnyness going east. From any raised viewpoint, they peel off both east and west in parallels; parallel table-top headlands, parallel low hills which dip seaward like lolling tongues, parallel black rock staircases, their ground-floor landings awash with parallel seas.

The symmetry of two such staircases was suddenly and wonderfully flawed when an otter appeared on the second bottom step of the nearer one. There she devoured some species of dogfish with all the relish of the sea's devouring of the land. Waves drenched otter and prey but the otter ate unflinchingly until the prey dwindled to uselessness and she gave it carelessly back to the sea. She turned then, dropped to the bottom step. Would she then go tripping on down those stepped rocks which climbed on down below the tide, carrying her amphibiousness to such pointless extremes? She threw me a long glance of inquisition, stepped off to draw her own conclusions. And no, she did not walk downstairs through the tide. She swam.

An untutored mind shipwrecks itself on the imponderable conundrums which litter such an ancient shore like skerries. One particularly tutored mind, Professor R.J. Berry, yields up this one, for example, in his remarkably lucid book, *The Natural History of Shetland*: '(The rocks) were already in existence in very much the same state as now, long before the Caledonian mountains started to form. Several thousand million years ago they would have been granites intruded by small bodies of gabbro. Then they were recrystallised and deformed deep in the earth's crust and transformed into gneisses....'

My own untutored mind wrestles with that idea, the geological leopard changing its spots, and gawps at the prospect of the forces at work. I know the character of such rocks only as surfaces to climb on. I think of how hand and mind respond to the different psychologies of climbing in the Cairngorms (granite), the Cuillin (gabbro), the Harris hills (gneiss), and I try and think of how one landform might plunge into the earth's core and climb again to re-emerge as another, quite transformed in shape and colour, texture and character, and all over a matter of a handful of thousands of millions of years. Your head begins to hurt when you try to think about what the particular rock you stand on might have been through before you got there. And yet, you console yourself, if a seal can step ashore as a beautiful maiden and woo a land-thirled man seawards, why shouldn't a rock dive deep and resurface new and uncanny? There are times when it is more restful to side with the poets of the land.

Still, in the darkest fastness of Shetland's oldest rock, Shetland's newest bird was hewing away at the inside of an eggshell, while its mother stirred to the small tremor beneath her. What emerged was a nestling which was born looking ancient, as prehistoric as the rock ledges which spawned it, a small, brown unfeathered monstrosity (a shag, we can't all be swans), but life for all that. Furthermore, it was a true Shetlander, and where better for a true Shetlander to stumble chin-first into the sea-bright light of day? What privileges of lineage, what fey powers might rub off on such a Shetlander brooded and weaned and fledged in such a monumental cradle?

I retreated above the shore partly to avoid disturbing the new-born shag, partly to prowl my instincts around the ruined crofts on the hill (called Uyea after the island at the corner of the coast). It is a disappointingly prosaic name for such a setting, no more than an extreme corruption of 'Øy', the Norse for an isle. Here I confronted the same questions, found the ruins no more than a literal translation of the shag's roofless home. Were these ruins, too, hewn out of the oldest rocks in Shetland? Were their inhabitants likewise blessed by knowledge and instincts which reached down through eons to the beginnings of all Shetland's time? It is far from fanciful to carry a torch for the idea that the powers of landscape can illuminate and colour the minds of those who are born in and inhabit the very cradle of that landscape. Build one house in the old island tradition from the doorstep stone which has evolved itself through nature's tumultuous tradition; build another with complete disregard for landscape setting and tradition, with new-minted brick or breeze blocks and acres of glass; step slowly from one to the other, and if you find no presence in one and no absence of moulding characteristics in the other, you are less than stone yourself. You are brick, perhaps, or breeze block, or double-glazed against the subtleties and sensitivities of the true Shetland.

Look at that gable end of Uyea. It is a wall to watch from within through all its island lights: peat flame, storm-dark, simmer dim. It is moulded in its building not by dimensions and regularities and mathematics and kit house limitations, but by the fact of its curved hearthstone. The whole wall bows and bends away from verticals and horizontals with a gentle flexibility because it must accommodate that single wide curved stone. A straight one would have been much more practical, of course, and doubtless its first mason would have used one if one had fallen to hand. But who knows the circumstances of necessity or whim which dictated that crucial curve? Besides, a straight one would have built less of a wall. It would have been an easy wall to live with, for sure.

So too, the setting of Uyea. The eyes of the houses are long blinded, crudely stone-shuttered by a lesser hand, but the doorway still gazes wide and tirelessly north-east past the stuttering headland of Fethaland to the Ramna Stacs...Gruney, Flae-ass, Fladda, Turla, Scordar, Outer Stack, Gaut Skerries. Who last pronounced that sunwise litany? How long gone? Who first? How long between first and last? I see a mother and child stand in that slim doorway, black against the smouldering simmer-dim fires, the child's mind and tongue grappling with the far procession of rocks, the woman's approving glance as the child reaches 'Gaut Skerries' for the first unhesitating time. The child would carry that first-name familiarity with the rock tribe throughout his life's world, and summon it whenever his voyagings alighted on the outer shores of their worlds, or whenever his mind's eye contrived the vision of a wind-bright sea. But what of today's island child? What vision does he cling to? His Shetland has turned its back on Uyea, withdrawn from almost all its outposts (the number of populated islands has halved in the last 100 years), seduced by the centralised culture of more southerly influences. If it does not learn to resist that seduction, Shetland will deny the child his true heritage, his sunwise litany of stacks. Who will delve again along the land of the outer shore? Who will scrape the thin mossy turf away from the old cobbled floor of Uyea, set a new roof on its walls and a burning peat in its hearth?

I retraced the day's steps deep and dark within myself for all the swamping brightness of Uyea on the hill and the glittering ocean-going showers. The uprooting of that Shetland which was and the withering of its bloom can cloud the mind. Such withering is a familiar enough process throughout the ocean islands of Europe, although in Shetland of all places with its quiet and assured self-containment, it seems particularly conspicuous. It is easy to romanticise about the ways which were, of course, especially on an island, and few landscapes fuel romance like Shetland, but there is more to it than that. It is the heart of an island which falters when its most intimate associations with the landscape are forfeited. There is so much about Shetland which is instantly and recognisably characteristic, but the forces of change and smothering anonymity are a heady momentum which no society has ever found easy to resist. When the change is accelerated by oil, as Shetland's has been these last few giddy decades, the question begins to lean towards not how much can survive, but how little. The ruin of Uyea is a small symbol, but it is only its location which is isolated. It would be a foolish man who would argue that change has brought no benefits to the islanders, but there is much which was distinctively and definitively Shetland which the forces for change have either ignored, or discarded or both.

Birds tumbled across my eastering tracks. Arctic skuas - variously referred to as aalins, skooty aalins, allens, or skooties - chased the winds. Golden plovers smothered hill and moor and shore with song like dew. It is not so much the plumage of the birds which is golden but the music. It is such a pervasive call of Shetland's wilder acres that you wonder at its absence from that Shetlandic roll-call of birds. Ravens slouched along the cliffs, diving down on the sitting fulmars - maalies - trying to prize them from their eggs, but mostly, the fulmars which took flight were just sitting, not brooding, and a brooding fulmar has a particularly vile form of self-defence - it spits a stinking, cloying oil - which doubtless the ravens are as aware of as anything which walks or flies that shore. So the ravens threw black oaths after the fliers, venting their disappointment on a furious chase down to the sea and back. And every raven, skua and fulmar which strayed too far inland was met with fired salvos of golden plover and lapwing, delectably sung arias of protest.

It is that time of year, the heart of this Shetland spring, when a kind of irrational fever - like the boxing of hares - overtakes the bird world, and in Shetland, where birds are so much a part of the pageant of the land, the fever is an epidemic. Every mile of that shore was a clamouring controversy, every other yard a territory defended or encroached, every step an adventure which cried out for a denouement. It all had its headiest moment back where I started, in the bay of the divers, the eiders and the rest. Only the eiders remained now, two ducks, two drakes, folded and dozing on the shore like matching sets of pebbles. As I contoured down the headland to their shore, they stirred and stepped unhurriedly onto the water, where a perfunctory snap of a drake's beak on the lime-green nape of the other's neck, stung the birds like a bell to boxers. The contest which followed bore all the hallmarks of the resumption of earlier hostilities, for there were no preliminary skirmishings. For the next half hour, the drakes warred and threshed the inshore water into a tormented arena while the females first swam away in apparent alarm, only to wheel and pose and watch addictively, held in the magnetic forcefield of battle. The nature of the combat seemed to evolve round grabbing the other drake by the neck and forcing it underwater, a ritualised attack presumably when you consider how little damage might be inflicted on such an ocean-diving duck as an eider by forcing it underwater. Every bout was bafflingly interspersed with periods of calm, during which all four birds consorted as convivially as bridge partners, until one drake strayed or steered too near the other and all feather-flying hell broke loose again.

It resolved itself as quickly as it began. The females became suddenly unenthralled and stepped ashore. The drakes stepped grandly after them, and sat, folded pebbles again, licking wounds, unruffling feathers, stoking prides, smooring the fires of the season for the moment at least. Suddenly that old Shetlandic word 'dunter' which once you judged brutal, seemed an unwarranted and misplaced expression of moderation.

Back in the axehead of the voe, I found the other eiders, four drakes agog at a single duck, nothing more physical than the aawhoo-ing croon and the posturing toss of heads. Nothing so crude as a dunter in sight. The voe echoed and echoed to their overtures, the waters flat and unforbidding. The oldest rocks in Shetland and their sea-and-seabird frenzies seemed a world away instead of a mile, but such is the way of Shetland on the land of the outer shore.

If you are addicted to whetting the appetite of a journey by poring through maps and fitting imaginary landscapes to unfamiliar names, you will find much in the four O.S. sheets covering Shetland to slake your addiction. What will you make of Fitful Head, the Slithers, Giltarump, Gloup, The Faither, Tongan Swarta, Grind o'da Navir, Sneck o'da Smaalie? Better still, what will you make of The Drongs? Who or what were or was (or God forbid, still are!) the Drongs, and what dire moment in Shetland's history caused a monument to be struck to mark their passing? The mind's eye roves around the idea of an Iron Age tribe, perhaps a Pictish sect? On second thoughts, the name carries overtones of unpleasantness, like a bovine disorder. ('We had to put down a whole herd – it was the drongs. Nothing else to be done.') Or a species of sea monster like a selkie with dragon's breath? The reality, like so much of Shetland's captivating nomenclature, is less bizarre. It is not that The

Drongs do not have powers to captivate, it is just that they are rocks, and their name, for all its overtones and undertones, means, well...rocks.

Ah, but what rocks! They are the climactic exclamation mark to a ragged ellipsis of lesser rocks and stacks which strut out from the Ness of Hillswick into St.Magnus Bay, standing stones of the ocean, or a red granite Canute wading waist deep and still urging the tide into retreat. From every angle and in every light, The Drongs effect their own cosmetics subtly made up in red or gold or gray or black; reconstituting themselves from this airt or that - a Marie Celeste reincarnation, a lofty cloaked brotherhood in secretive whispered committee (and chaired, I fancy, by the Head Drong), an uncanny Viking helmet from the bay's north shore (where the coast pronounces its own tangy vocabulary...The Runk, Stoura Pund, Heads of Grocken, Harry's Pund, Gray Face...).

I tramped out the Ness of Hillswick on a morning brimming with all May's promise. The moorland score of birdsong swung with a jazzy vigour buoyed on big bright winds, layered by soprano larks, whoopfuls of lapwing oboe sound, driven by the erratic rhythms of oystercatchers, curlew and rock-percussionist wheaters (called staneychaakers, the best of all Shetlandic bird names). Beyond all that, and where the sea was loudest, kittiwakes shrilled a quiet chorale. Kittiwakes are rippacks here, the one Shetland name which doesn't improve on the name I grew up with. Kittiwake has always seemed the perfect name for what it is, the perfect onomatopoeic accompaniment to the perfect wild island shore. The Drongs lay close at hand now, and I spent an energetic hour or two walking up to the highest point of the Ness, the westmost point, the southmost point, and from each of these, rearranging the rocks into new shapes and orders. The right-hand Drong detaches itself as you walk south, stands free and slender and high as a redwood pine, but the left-hand stack separates only at the root, not the branch, no matter how far you walk.

Finally I gave up on the rock-moving game and just sat high on the cliffs at Oris Field, watched The Drongs while away half a day until the sky-fires dowsed, the wind slackened, and an eastering layer of cloud crawled low across the ocean, and the bay dragged down smirry irritations of rain. The Drongs, so red in the morning light, drained to a dull gray gleam, and when I took my leave of them, it was not a helmet or a Canute or a cabal or a phantom ship I left behind but sea-wearied rocks, stripped of their illusory powers by the killjoy cloud, sullen, steely and shrunken. But late in the evening, I climbed the Watch Hill to test my instincts on a far paling of the western sky. From the hilltop, I watched it play down the sea over perhaps half an hour, alight about the sea roots of The Drongs, and as it lit the rocks anew they flared and glowed, the Viking helmet restored, and fashioned not from granite but gold.

The northern shore of St. Magnus Bay is rimmed by the headland of Eshaness with its inevitable lighthouse (Shetland has lighthouses round every corner, an erratic blinking candelabra of the dusk). The shore, if you catch it on a certain day, is a place of two spectacles, or rather a single spectacle with two component parts – a day-long procession of gannets north-ing it up the rim of the ocean, and the architectural wizardry the ocean has styled and re-styled from tortured miles of cliffs. However your eye lingers on the gannets or the rocks, the one will find a new way to interrupt your awe or your admiration of the other, until you finally learn that they are indivisible and ease a little more into their company.

A wind-blunting perch among these rocks, as high and sea-daring as you can stomach, unfurls the gannets at eye-level, sometimes almost within touching distance. They pass in haphazard groupings, twos and threes, sixes and sevens, dozens, scores, while long, low-slung and undulating skeins parallel their journey, far out up the open sea. The low fliers seem to work harder for their flight, the cliff-huggers hold hard to the thermals and the buffeting winds and ride their unseen switchbacks, long-striding commuters to and from the fishing grounds, enslaved to the fickle demands of their prey. It is a stylish procession. Gannets are slim, snow-bright, yellow-helmeted, pencil-winged, ocean lanced. Concorde elegance is undermined only by a stage-propish glass eye with too much eye shadow. The young birds go dowdily among them as if a motley rag-bag of tramps had blundered into a mannequin parade. By the third year of immaturity, the birds' plumage has achieved such a bizarre weave of the old and the transitional and the new that the effect is rather of a fashion experiment gone disastrously wrong. Still, they fly serenely enough.

Shoal after shoal, hour after hour, the birds traipse north, a disciplined uniformity about their flight which is the appeal of all seabird spectacle. It is like having a favourite passage from a favourite symphony played over and over again, and with every new playing, a little more understanding, a little more appreciation of its beauty unfolds. Not one bird flies south, not one heedless of the communal command, 'North!' The only variations on that symphonic theme are inshore and offshore, and even then the cliff-huggers carve their white wedge out into the wake of the ocean-goers as soon as they run out of shore.

Lesser travellers drift through the flowing tide of gannets, eye-balling fulmars, sleekly discreet common gulls, a caterwaul of kittiwakes, beavering puffins. It is a congested airspace for basement dwellers to negotiate, but a single shag, vivid green in that press of white and gray, manoeuvres a landing with some style. The bird approaches from the sea at shearwater level, pulls back at a climb as steep as a cliff up the seaward flank of the gannets, wheels high above them two circles peerie-wise, spies a lull in their procession, loops down through it on stiff dragon wings, celebrates the execution of the manoeuvre by a complete circuit of the cove with wings unflinching, primevally heraldic, then vanishes into a secret niche of the cliff. Such is the artistry and the bravado of the homing flight that you feel you should applaud.

The gannets resume. On and on they come and on and on they go. When the shag takes to the sea again, it simply drops from a ledge and beats a wavetop beeline beneath the thickening white convoy, which makes you wonder why it didn't arrive that way. Was the arrival style necessary, or simple exhibitionism? Necessary or not, it was worth the watching. On and obliviously on go the solans.

So I paralleled my own passage to theirs, walking up the shore of the Villians of Ure where the clifftop sward is stippled with lochans and punctuated with geological eccentrics like the Holes of Scraada. There, where the sea comes ashore 50 yards inland and twice as many feet below your clifftop gaze, you watch gingerly. It is the rocks beneath the sward I have come here to see, however, so I thread an equally gingering descent (any exploration of Shetland's outer shore is well spiced with ginger) to that underworld of the ocean edge which the clifftop miles only hint at and belittle.

At sea level, the rocks intimidate. They loom fantastically and in every shape and shade. After the far horizons of the clifftop, there are suddenly no horizons, only the rumpled advance of the ocean, the wilting buffer of the rocks. In the midst of that strewment of monoliths, and on the front line of that oldest of battlefields, I feel as inconsequential and fleeting as a fly on the wall of a broch. It is good to be here, but it is not a constructive pursuit to dwell on the ephemerality of human life – or fly's – in the face of such eon-endurance.

The clifftop, it now emerges, is the flat roof of cloisters. The sea has bitten deep and undercut the cliff face into a subterranean passage shored up by stubborn pillars and pedestals which the waves found easier to circumnavigate than devour. They are hardly the kind of cloisters where you can go with contemplative monk-like calm, however. Not only is the sea rarely far from the cloister floor even at its lowest ebb, but the floor is littered with the vast debris which the sea has wrenched from walls or ceiling, or heaved up from the foreshore.

Scale is everything in the appreciation of such a shore. Right down at rock bottom, a yard above the sea, you are David surrounded by armies of Goliaths, and the slingshot of your mind's best defence is crudely overwhelmed, a puny armoury. A rock arch, for example, juts vastly out from the cliff face, but much of the time, it is not rooted in the sea. It is thus an arch of rock springing from cliff rock to foreshore rock over a rock thoroughfare going nowhere. On the bravest of bright spring days, it is the blackest of places. The first sight of it lodges a catch in your throat. But scramble to the apex (more ginger) of a rough rock pyramid, and the elevation of perhaps 30 feet puts you at waist level, or eye-level or head and shoulders above the shore's sculptures, and things fall into a cooler, airier order. From here, too, the sun strikes a glittering eye of light in the blackness of the arch, and you see it for what it is, a tortured and fraying fragment of the shore. Of all that coast's perpetual procession of seabirds, though, not one dared the arch, not even the shags with their perverse delight in the dankest, dingiest alcoves of the shore. I watched that arch off and on for two hours, which is a long time to watch a rock, and even from my crow's nest on the pyramid and even with the sun striking a glimmer in its eye, it never shed its shuddering aspect. I found nowhere else in Shetland with such an intimidating presence, nowhere else, no matter how troubled the shoreline, which was not redeemable by some trick of the light or shade or sun or snow. Surely this black arch of Eshaness is the monument to a dire sorrow?

A year after that first encounter, Colin Baxter and I returned to Eshaness to watch the play of a mighty gale along the shore. Stacks and skerries and cliff faces we had marvelled at and walked along the previous spring were now inundated by these frenzies of the ocean, so hugely overwhelmed that the scene bore no credible resemblance to the shore we remembered. The ocean charged the base of the cliffs and heaved itself 100 feet up the faces, or gatecrashed the darkest alleys and crannies with its furious white ocean light. The kittiwakes revelled in it, dived down from their echo-chamber ledges to skip and cry and laugh always just above the highest thrust of the storm.

The black arch came into my mind then, invisible from where we sat, and quite unapproachable in these conditions. Seas like these would be breaking right over it, whitewashing its blackness, rubbing salt into the wounds of its eternal sorrows. It will take one such sea to bring the whole mass to its knees, to let light and life into one fragment of the shore which has starved of both for centuries. I wish the storms of Eshaness well in their efforts.

SOMETHING IN the way this shore piles one rock sensation on top of another smacks of a Jarlshof ordered by nature, storeys of the sea's masonry, the oldest rocks re-worked, re-ordered, redesigned into new shapes and purposes and structures, just as at Jarlshof, men took the stones of the old to build anew, again and again over thousands of years. It was that 16th-century laird's house called 'Sumburgh' by the Shetlanders of its heyday which Scott re-christened and wove into *The Pirate*, but he was so unsuspecting of what lay beneath that

he confidently wrote it off as 'a rude building of rough stone with nothing about it to gratify the eye or to excite the imagination'. Well, the eye is much gratified now by the multi-storeyed labyrinth which has emerged from Sumburgh's millenia of sandstorms and swaddling peat. And just as a low tide on the Eshaness coast briefly unravels new underwater mysteries, so this low tide of discarded sand and peat sets the mind racing after even older secrets which may yet emerge beneath those collective civilisations we have come to call Jarlshof. The imagination is as excitable here as the eye is gratified, and oh the novels a Scott might have written if only he had known what it was the laird borrowed the stone from when he set down his house!

Not even the wretched pervasiveness of the Department of the Environment monotones and compulsory clipped lawns can corrupt the sense of wonder which clings like lichen about the deepest recesses of Jarlshof. (But how much more Shetland-like it would feel if the flowers and grasses were given their head!) Watch the sun work its way round the buttresses of the wheelhouse like a sundial, shadowing some, glistening others. Think of the hands which worked so assuredly, dismantling broch and courtyard, re-laying stones which had already served man and beast well for thousands of years, demonstrating a skill the broch builders would certainly have admired. The passage house, a sort of 'ben' to the wheelhouse's 'but', is entered through a door of such tiny Alice-in-Wonderland proportions that you half expect to find a bottle in an alcove bearing the words 'drink me'.

Sumburgh's appeal for the tribes of history and pre-history is not hard to fathom, a key site on the southmost tip of Shetland with a natural harbour, much good stone, fresh water, and – by Shetland standards at least – fertile soil for crops and grazing animals. So what if the sea and its winds breached a wall here or there or billowed sand infuriatingly in the face of this enterprise or that? Sumburgh, for all its storm-flaws, was better than much which lay to the north.

The surprise is that it all ground to a halt when it did, for the Sumburgh which Scott found in 1814 was already ruinous. The 19th-century Sumburgh House, now a hotel, stands at a remove from the sea, and from the Shetlandness of Jarlshof. It is a place as apart from its landscape as Jarlshof is uniquely immersed.

The airport has hardly added to modern Sumburgh's appeal, for all that it has become a crucial element in Shetland's economic miracle. You cannot fossilise the island way of life – the developing and redeveloping of successive civilisations at Jarlshof itself underline the truth – and if the distancing of Shetlanders from much of the land of the outer shore is a trait of modern Shetland it is no different from many an isolated land trying to come to terms with the end of the 20th-century. Still, it is sad that it should happen on this, of all headlands. Shetland life lives on at its distinctively Shetland best where it still lights a hearth on its stormiest shores, but it is a frail flame and fading.

WINTER, AS described to me by a crewman on the Unst ferry, was 'gales and gales and gales', so he had more right than I do to relish the blue flat calm, the sky as shorn of fleece as a summer ewe, the sun which was well up by six and wouldn't be down till past nine at night, and the second half of April only a week old. Still, it's a long time to wait for the first hint of spring. He shot the sun a squint. 'We deserve this,' he said.

I wonder what I did to deserve Muckle Flugga in the same flat calm, but there it was, the sea so untroubled that the lighthouse buildings threw a white sheen down through the water, not a reflection so much as a hint of a presence. But who would have thought such a thing was possible off the northmost point of the northmost point of the land (and technically the northmost point of Scotland and Britain, although there is little of either Scottishness or Britishness here)? Muckle Flugga is the offshore afterthought to Hermaness, famed seabird colony and gathering point for all the winds of the northern hemisphere. There are many tales of birdwatchers crawling across that turbulent headland and treading fearfully towards the rim of its gannetry. I had just crossed it stripped to the waist and sun-burdened, to sit above the lighthouse and among the puffins. The first conscious sense which imposed itself was one of unreality.

Hermaness, then, is far enough for most mortals, but every school pupil and Trivial Pursuitist will tell you that Muckle Flugga is the most northerly fragment of the British Isles, and that after that there is nothing. Wrong. The northmost tip of the northmost tip is a drab little gray wedge of bird-scorned rock with the supremely mundane name of Out Stack. It sounds more like an orange than a fingerpost to the Arctic. Out Stack also has the distinction of being the first mark at the top of Sheet One of the Ordnance Survey maps of Britain, and seemingly so far north that they had to break into the margin at the top of the map to accommodate it. Did they forget? Tch, tch, bad start.

The birds, and particularly the gannets, so overwhelm the last of the land in the breeding season, that winter with no more than a smattering of drab young birds for company and the imprisoning forces of 'gales and gales and gales' must have inflicted unimaginable desolations on generations of lighthouse keepers. There must have been weekfuls of dire days in the worst of their winters, the spirit-sapping trial of ceaseless storm. How they must have greeted the birds' return as celebrations of ritual! Company! Puffins for the gladdest company (and among the last arrivals), gannets for the most garrulous and best-dressed, fulmars for the boldest blinking by your head, kittiwakes for the most

eloquently conversational. Discount the bonxies. They may go gannet-bashing out over the sea, and they are aggressive to a fault on the headland, but not even a bonxie is up to staking a territorial claim to Muckle Flugga light.

Muckle Flugga is the second top of the league table of islands and stacks, topped by Out Stack. Second bottom, and counterbalancing the archipelago is the gannetry of the rock called Rumblings. Reekings would be better, especially in the warm promise of such a day. The white buildings around the lighthouse (the tower itself is pinkish) are offset by the packed whiteness of the granite of the gannets of Rumblings. In that April sunlight, the gannetry is at its most aesthetically perfect, none of the towsy chicks yet or the immatures in their freaky piebalds, but a drifting whitewash of mature adults in pristine breeding plumage. They stand and sit and doze and sun themselves, they come and go, they grapple and mate, and all day they chatter and scold and croon and caress and stink. It is as perfect as any gannetry gets.

Shetland is forever playing its vast repertoire of tricks on those who come to scrutinise its landscapes. You march across Hermaness anticipating hurricanes, tastes of the Arctic, icebergs maybe! Instead there is an ocean which is positively lagoonish, and gannets panting away the heat. Bonxies lie on their noon-tide couches and blink disinterestedly. So this is Thule?

It is a fluke, of course, and most other days of the year, there is no mistaking the northness of where you stand. Shetland is a place of the north, and this, its northmost gesture, should speak to you in rarified tones, just as there is a westmost significance to St.Kilda. Sumburgh would be nothing without Jarlshof, other than a symbolic reunion for homing Shetlanders, but Hermaness is everything because it is the last of the north of this northmost land. If, as I do, you adhere instinctively to things of the north like tundra moss and whooper swans and sagas, it is enough to be alive on the day Hermaness flattered to deceive and welcome. By and large, it is not the blue days of life I cherish (a positive discrimination which Colin Baxter and I share and which adds to the many satisfactions of our joint ventures), but the day I came on Looss Wick of Hermaness as tranquil as the sands of St. Ninian's Isle is one that time will not lightly shut out.

I have one more abiding memory of Muckle Flugga, burned like a scar on my mind. It is that the lighthouse rock is scaled from sea level to summit by a man-made staircase, dead straight in eight or nine flights, each of perhaps 30 steps, which with the squat rectangular buildings around the light suggest the kind of result you might get if you asked the Ministry of Defence to design a temple. It is a graphic fragment of the lighthouse keeper's life, for how those steps must have been cursed in their time (or blessed perhaps on the bottom rung of the last descent of a tour of duty). Dreams have been haunted by those steps, so that they become a hundred flights, a thousand, and the light perched on a stair-cased Ben Nevis. It is no meagre tribe of men who tended the Muckle Flugga light, first and last symbol of the land of the outer shore.

IT WOULD be convenient, as well as symbolic, to uphold Muckle Flugga and Hermaness as the great showpiece of the outer shore, but for all its boreal significance, it is outshone in many places. When I think of that duologue of rock and ocean in which Shetland sings its most seductive song, I think first of a bitten red-granite shore at the bottom end of that west-facing arrowhead of the Shetland mainland which the islanders call the Westside. This is Westerwick, a three-ringed circus with a capacity to make you gasp aloud to an empty headland at the astounding sequence of its performers. Westerwick itself is the centrepiece of all this, a fantastic pink-walled horseshoe of the ocean, as glorious a definition of that Shetland word 'wick' as you could wish for. Wick is pronounced 'week' and derives from the Norse 'vik', and according to John Stewart's remarkable labour-of-love book, *Shetland Place Names*, 'the correspondence is to the word "bight" rather than "bay"'. The Official Tourist Map has either not read Mr. Stewart or does not believe him, for it lists 'Westerwick Bay', which by my calculation translates as 'west bight bay', and that makes very little sense in any language. As bights go, Westerwick's cliffs are tiled with the teethmarks of the ocean, its sea surface littered with crunched fragments of the land. It is not beautiful so much as mighty. At the slackest of tides on the calmest of days, it is not peace which reigns but an impatient tension, eager for resumed hostilities.

The glare of a long hot afternoon takes its toll. One huge buttress on the west side of the Wick assumes the shape of the head of a hush puppy with its nose and the ends of its ears in the water. Two more equidistant buttresses are its paws. It's such a good likeness you catch yourself laughing out loud to no-one. But then the light shifts, your mind's eye seeks out more mischief, and by throwing a wider angle further out along the cliffs, the hush puppy becomes the head and torso of an eagle, the tapering cliffs a mighty downbeat of wings. Now a light is flickering on and off in the darkest corner of the base of the cliffs, not a regular pulse like a lighthouse (and anyway why would a lighthouse trickle its light into such a flood of sunshine?) but a haphazard gleam, just above the dark blur of the beach. It is tempting to write it off as a trick of the ocean light, but it niggles away in a corner of an eye like an itch you cannot scratch until its riddle demands to be solved. Closer inspection through the glasses reveals that what seems like a flank of unbroken cliff is actually the

protruding wall of a small geo. The sea has eaten a tiny arch into the wall of the geo, and the light is the sun striking on a single breaking wave in the geo, but visible through the arch in its side-wall. From any other spot on the rim of the Wick, other than the precise rock where I sit, the 'light' is invisible. How often the outer shore throws up such conundrums, and the whiling away of an hour there is punctuated by the fascination of solving them. The light is also a clue to the fact that there is more to Westerwick than this single compelling horseshoe of rock and trapped ocean. How much more emerges with startling suddenness as you walk south down the Westerwick headland of Lambigart, where you crest what looks like nothing more than a rise in the ground to find that one more step would take you into the sea 300 feet below you, and that your eyes are dancing across a new arena of the sea.

Here the shore is more bay than bight, a ragged south-eastering three-mile curve, and populated with a repertoire of stacks which suggest that the sculptors of Europe experimented wildly here before they finally settled on the principles of Gothic architecture. Their best effort is a rough spire, perhaps 150 feet high, crudely lopsided, but with a kittiwake perched perfectly in the weathercock position. It recalls the Inaccessible Pinnacle of the Skye Cuillin in every aspect but colour, and the fact that it is rooted in the sea rather than into a 3,000-feet high mountain ridge. Inevitably, the ocean is making inroads into the root of the stack, wearing away a small cave which will become an arch, until one tide too many prises away a last loosening fragment and the whole trembling spire totters down to the seabed.

For now, the Gothic stack dominates a small inner wick, beyond which the shore widens only to be barred by two vast stacks, one the daunting and uncanny shape of Liathach of Wester Ross, the other a small replica of Table Mountain (the stacks of the Outer Shore have a contemptuous way with the geography of the world). It is altogether a staggering gathering of rocks, and there is as much more of it to the west of Wester Wick as there is to the east. My headland cranes far enough out into the sea and inclines far enough back towards the well-stacked shore to give the impression of an offshore view of the ocean's assault on the rock. If Eshaness was a wick rather than a ness it might throw you such a perspective of the ocean's incomprehensible labours.

It is the oldest Shetland story of them all, yet no matter how often you see and hear its single drama re-enacted, there is no tiring of it. Then, when you think you've seen and heard it all, and the land of the outer shore holds no more surprises for you, board a ferry or a plane for Foula, and on that skyline island's north shore hear and see the story rewritten as you could never have believed it. But first there are gentler lands to explore.

Chapter Three

THE LAND OF THE INNER SHORE

THE CLUTCH of the Norse-tongued names which cling to the slopes and hills around Gunnister Voe are as unambiguous as the landscape. Setter of Enisfirth, the Vaava, Virdins of Hamar, Soolmis Vird, Gruna, Nibon, Smirna Dale, Snapa Water...their wide vowels and rhythmic gutturals as rooted in the landscape as geos and gloups and stacks. Even where elements of English have insinuated into a name, like Snowbuil, you find that recent history's preference was for Snabuil or Snaebol, that at the root of the word is 'bol', a resting place for animals. John Stewart translates Snowbuil endearingly as 'a place where sheep were folded in snowstorms'. It is no coincidence that with the ocean raging icily beyond the Isle of Nibon at the mouth of Gunnister Voe, Snowbuil on the voe flank is almost wind-free and mild-aired. You can envisage no wind which could inflict much suffering on the folded sheep, for all Shetland's voes calm as they burrow inland, often bending away from the lie of prevailing winds. Gunnister is extra blessed by the Isle of Nibon and the Isle of Gunnister lodged benevolently in its sea-jaw, and in the steely leeward waters between the islands and the shore and the eastering voe flanks are assembled all the elements you could wish for to begin an exploration of the land of the inner shore. Mostly, such a landscape is the work of melting ice, the sea level rising unusually quickly, drowning river valleys and fashioning islands from hills. There the sea lies, trapped by its own avarice, and while it hammers the outer shore into all manner of tortured submissions, it is meek and mild and impotent on the inner shore. It also makes for some of Shetland's most compelling and beautiful landscapes.

Thick layers of cloud have built up through the morning, but high and unmenacing, and sunlight still darts among them, prises apart or punches through for seconds or moments at a time. All this glitters and fades on the water while cloud shadows shade and shine the hills in fast patchworks. The terns dart through the moving light or flicker down onto the sand at the head of the voe, and even their whiteness is vivid and pallid by degrees of the light's trickery. The water itself shifts barely perceptibly through every shade of gray from almost white to almost black, the shades drifting and mingling as though countless underwater shoals were prowling the depths of the voe, rising to just below the surface then plummeting deep again, taking the pale stain of their mass down with them. Such days are the reward for the landscape watcher in a land of so many winds. Much of the time, you curse the wind for its unwearying tenacity, but here where it tap-dances in tandem with a fitful sun on the waters of the voe, it works tireless magic.

A tiny unnamed island lies beneath Snowbuil like a green pancake. Across the voe is one more of Shetland's township ruins, surrounded by the purposeful declaration of its old headwall. The headwall climbs the hill, contours high above the ruins, descends to the shore again, a pointed labour once so crucial to the wellbeing of the Shetlanders of Gunnister Voe, now useless and unkempt, keeping nothing out and nothing in place. I feel here, among the arrayed beauties of the voe and the road to Nibon, the same regret I knew out at Uyea on the north shore by the oldest rocks. The thread of an age-old continuity is snapped. I linger long among such ruins as these above the shore of Gunnister Voe, because it takes little effort of the imagination to populate them with lives a few generations old, lives lived closer to the land, lives attuned to an older rhythm, lives which held their Shetlandness closer to themselves.

So I prospected among the ruins of a steading above the voe, and found in a small and roofless byre, not sickle or ploughshare or loom or harp, but the oldest motor cycle I have ever seen. The sea air had taken a voracious toll and so consumed every square millimetre of the surface metal with rust that no hint of the machine's colour survived. In a wall alcove lay a registration plate which had suffered the same fate. No flake of paint, no outline of lettering had survived. The saddle had springs, but only springs, the same orangey shade of rust as the rest. The tyres, a shade soft, still had a serviceable tread, but moss had risen from the peat to embed the wheels where they touched the ground. At a guess, it is perhaps 70 years old. At another, it has spent more than half that time waiting for someone to return. Who parked it, expecting to pick it up again in a day or two, or a month, or a year?

Perhaps it was the gleaming polished joy of a young mechanic who leaped at the chance to up the tired pace of island life by taking a few months off to stop Hitler in his menacing tracks. So one day, a day like this is, in the spring of 1940, he toured the bike back down from the house of a certain tearful Hillswick lass, parked it in the byre away from the bustle of the croft and found an old blanket to shroud it from the weather. Next day (more tears, a mother's and a fond sister's perhaps) he stepped down the road to the bus, to Lerwick, to the ferry, to the train, to the war. Perhaps he lay a month later, unshrouded, on Dunkirk's beach, and in that new flood of tears at Gunnister and Hillswick, the bike was forgotten, and so began its long, languishing sleep. A wheen of eager Shetland winters would make shreds of the blanket and the sea winds would invade the metal like conquering armies. Whatever its unfinished story, the motorbike waits and moulders while the voe fluctuates idly through decades of tides.

It was another year before I came down the road to Nibon again, the bike still there, unmoved, untouched, unexplained, uncollected. The registration plate was on its wall. The headwall of the township across the voe had wilted a little. Only a holiday house out at Nibon wore fresh paint. It is easy to see why a young man eager for adventure might stride purposefully to the pulse of a snare drum and the throb of a far war, far from the quietude of a small and withering valley.

That weave of Gunnister Voe's two islands, their North and South Sounds, the calm of the voe and the audible hammering of the sea a headland away, the chaotic incisions of seabird flight...all that conveys a frantic edge about the tranquillity of Nibon. There is a perpetual boisterous weeping and wailing of birds, for there are few silences and little discretion among the seabird tribes, and when the principals are such a definitively Shetland trilogy as tirricks, bonxies and shaldurs, you wonder how anyone could have conceived the bizarre idea of nature as a fount of harmony and order and balance. Yet the warring of the birds is waged on a landscape set of such stark appeal that it is easy to see only the beauties of the flights, not a ritual of survival; something choreographed or symphonically scored, not the wildest instinct of nature.

I watched through a long morning as the small bay between island and shore slowly filled with terns, much as a mountain corrie fills with snow, the first flakes presaging the deluge. The tide had brought with it a meagre bounty of sand eels, staple diet for much of Shetland's seabird hordes, and as the shoal surfaced, the bird-snow fell. Every sand eel plucked from the water had to be strenuously defended through dizzying chases, tirrick versus tirrick, until the fisher bird either caught its breath long enough to swallow its catch or was coerced into dropping it, in which case there was invariably one more scarlet gullet agape to catch it before it hit the water, and a new chase was unleashed. Even swallowing the fish is no guarantee of keeping it, because bonxies cruise the drifts of birds, and their worst attentions can persuade tern or gannet or osprey or almost anything else which lives or chances on this shore to regurgitate a fish in return for a moment's peace. It will be intriguing to watch how brave or foolhardy the bonxies might become if the great shadow of the sea eagle ever darkens Shetland summers again.

In this company, however, not even the bonxies have it all their own way. They are repeatedly mauled by the flashing lances of bands of musketeer birds, terns and oystercatchers mostly. It is an even contest of eight or ten musketeers to one bonxie – even, that is, for everything but the sand eel, which is everyone's prize.

Alas for the wellbeing of bird and fish, it has also become man's prize. The damage inflicted on the sand eel population of Shetland's waters coincides with the growth through the 1980s of a new sand eel fishing industry in the islands, and although neither the fishermen nor the Department of Agriculture and Fisheries were satisfied that there was proof enough to warrant a ban on sand eel fishing, the Royal Society for the Protection of Birds agitated long and loud for at

least a temporary ban, brandishing what any neutral observer could only conclude to be a very convincing body of evidence. It went something like this:

1974 – Sand eel fishing begins in Shetland. Early annual catches about 8,000 tonnes.

1982 – Annual catch now grown steadily to 52,000 tonnes.

1984 – A poor breeding season for Arctic terns alerts ornithologists to the fact that something is wrong.

1985 and 1986 – Complete breeding failure of Arctic terns, and fishermen's catches have slumped.

1987 – The RSPB and the Nature Conservancy Council fund a three-year study of Shetland bird colonies. The terns rear no chicks in any Shetland colony, but fare much better in Orkney and in Northumberland.

1988 – Researchers show that the largest tern colony in Shetland on Papa Stour has declined from 6,000 birds in 1980 to 1,500 birds, and estimate a similar decline throughout Shetland of 75%. The research intones:

Arctic skuas – 'very few young have been reared this year....'

Kittiwake – 'no chicks survived at any colonies on the east, south and south-west coast of Shetland. Complete breeding failure was noted at the major colonies of Noss (10,000 pairs), Sumburgh Head (2,000 pairs) and Foula (4,400 pairs).'

Puffin – 'large-scale breeding failure at Hermaness (25,000 pairs)...on Foula (48,000 pairs) almost total breeding failure....' These two colonies alone represent 10% of the British and Irish population.

Great Skua – 'the Shetland population in 1986 was 5,647 pairs, which represents 76% of the British population and 43% of the northern hemisphere population. At the largest colony (Foula) most chicks have died....'

1989 – A Cambridge marine biologist shows that the percentage of sand eels in the food puffins feed to their chicks has fallen from 100% (1973 to 1986) to 19% in 1987 and 36% in 1988. It is confirmed that Hermaness puffins raised no chicks in 1987 or 1988. The RSPB/NCC study shows another 'very poor season' with consequences similar to 1988 in terms of chicks fledged. About 100 tern chicks fledge in all Shetland, excluding Fair Isle where the only sizeable catches of sand eels are recorded, and breeding birds fare generally better. Two kittiwakes fledge from Noss's 10,000 pairs. Arctic skua fledging is the lowest ever recorded. Puffin chicks experience 'mass mortality', estimated 90% failure at Sumburgh Head, Hermaness and Foula. 'Most Arctic skua chicks died within 2-4 days of hatching and still retained the egg tooth...the demise of chicks was sudden and wholesale, and judging from the number of intact corpses, was due to food shortage rather than predation.' For the second year running, no chicks fledged from Papa Stour. Common and Arctic tern numbers have declined by

55% since 1980. 'Breeding success was almost non-existent for the sixth successive year.'

1990 – The RSPB calls for a temporary ban on sand eel fishing in Shetland, but the Department of Agriculture and Fisheries for Scotland concedes only a slight shortening of the season. On Noss, the vast kittiwake colony is noticeably smaller, the birds in poor condition, but the island is visited by record numbers of tourists who go to see the seabird colonies....

The RSPB warns: 'The sand eel fishery must remain closed for this year at least. Too high a catch now could jeopardise for years to come the sand eel itself and Shetland's internationally important breeding seabird colonies. We cannot afford to take chances. A continued ban will give stocks the chance to recover to a point where fishing can be sustained at a sensible level, to the long-term benefit of birds and fishermen alike.'

The Department's decision to permit fishing to carry on is based on 'scientific evidence'.

The Shetland Fish Producers Organisation votes against a ban. Both they, and the Department, need more proof before agreeing to a ban.

1991 – A total ban on sand eel fishing in Shetland waters. The RSPB announces that in 1990, 8,000 pairs of Arctic terns raised just two chicks; in 1991, 24,000 pairs produced at least 30,000 chicks. The society is cautious: 'The sudden abundance of sand eels this season is welcome, but it is not known what part the fishing ban played in this. Too little is known about sand eel populations and the ban must be maintained to allow the sand eels the maximum chance to recover and research to continue.'

1992 and beyond – The existence of the sand eel fishery is itself due to the retreat of inshore fishermen from traditional grounds where stocks have been wiped out by huge factory ships, thoughtlessly piratical, the bonxies of the industry. But it is surely clear – however much 'proof' may or may not be lacking – that for as long as the sand eels are at such a low ebb, the sea cannot be plundered forever without the discriminatory sense shown by many of our island forebears. It seems that the skills and judgments which balanced a good catch with the need to conserve fish stocks in the sea, have long been abandoned. The St. Kildans, who lived closer to the sea than most of us, set such an example in their consumption of sea birds and eggs, taking enough for their needs, but not permitting their needs to grow beyond what was necessary to sustain the birds' needs. There were many seeds which sowed the downfall of the St. Kildans, but failure of that fine judgment was not one of them.

Sand eels are not necessary to mankind. The industry processes most of them for pet food, so we can hardly argue in this case that by catching sand eels

we are attending to anything other than a pressing short-term economic difficulty of our own making. When that short-term expires (and it has come alarmingly close already) with the death of the last sand eel, we will not only have ensured permanent damage to the seabird colonies, but we may well have learned the hardest of lessons about the worth of the birds to us. Shetland's birds bring people to the islands, not just for the rarities which inevitably crop up on a stray wind, but for the spectacle of the bird hordes. People spend money, subsidise the ferries, sustain the economy and help to sustain the populations of the outlying islands. Without the bird spectacle, many will stay away. It is a big price to pay for the privilege of turning Shetland's sand eels into processed pulp.

None of that even begins to consider the rights of the birds themselves. They are, after all, older Shetlanders than the Shetlanders, and have a right to be, for their own sake. They are not here so that we can enjoy their spectacle. They are here, as we are, simply to be. But given that that right is one which we can uphold for them or snuff out, there has been a less than flattering self-interest about the industry's attitude throughout the controversy. It is true that there may well be natural phenomena at work which have dramatically influenced sand eel populations and movements but that possibility does not mitigate man's responsibility now. It may sound trite or naive or both to insist that for our own good as well as for nature's, we must suddenly stop accustomed practice. People have to live, after all, and in Shetland, many of them have to live from the sea. But it is as much of a truth that people also have to live with the sea and re-establish a harmony with which earlier eras were familiar, and which this one has abandoned. No-one reaps more than they sow, not farmer, not crofter, not fisherman. In the sand eel controversy, we can do nothing about natural phenomena. We can control how many we catch. The evidence of one fruitful season for the sand eels and the seabirds coinciding with the first year of a total ban on fishing is good circumstantial evidence but not proof. Perhaps only a tide of nature has turned, and the sand eels would have come back anyway. Perhaps. But there has to be a pact with nature, when our own wellbeing depends on its bounties too. In Shetland, and in the case of the sand eel, that means pause, concede, repair, heal, replenish. It can be done, for the forgiveness of nature is a force of exceptional generosity, but the first move must be ours.

It would be good to think that a lesson has already been learned, but the nature of man is rarely like that. Since the first restrictions were imposed on sand eel fishing in Shetland waters, a new sand eel fishery has burgeoned in the Minch. Already there are fears for the seabird populations of the Western Isles....

So the terns that fall on Nibon's South Sound have more reason than most to cling tenaciously to their silvery prey, the bonxies have more reason than most to harry it out of them. One of the bonxies' other sources of food is the great summer harvest of seabird chicks. In Shetland, without the sand eels, there are no chicks, not even bonxie chicks. It is a particularly vicious equation.

As I climbed away from the bay to the clifftops of Nibon, I wondered if the sand eel tribe had ever learned to come to terms with such a fate, one moment vigorous and alive and unsuspecting, and in their element, the next being helter-skeltered to death 50 feet above the water. I know they will not come to terms with a tin of cat food.

John Stewart translates Nibon as 'a height with a steep front' and that it undoubtedly is; in a matter of half an uphill mile the landscape transforms to a seascape. It is not the full ocean tumult of the outer shore, but one of those transitional coastlines which shepherd the sea between inner and outer shore, ocean and voe. The sea works the rock in more subtle ways hereabouts, with none of the flair and power of, say, Eshaness or the west coast of Papa Stour. It plays and sculpts on a smaller scale, struts a smaller stage. Watch how it whirls among the peaks of a tiny rock replica of Foula, perhaps ten feet across, catching its own tail as a new wave overwhelms the dribs and drabs of the old. Finally, as if nature as referee had decreed an end to the game, a surge of the tide threw a green veil over the rock, and the Foula that I had contrived for the purposes of the game was consigned to the oblivion of Atlantis. When you consider the mountain chain which Shetland once was, that small game of the sea and the rock was probably prophetic.

The sea has worked another small phenomenon here, slitting a narrow alley 70 or 80 yards into the rock, 50 feet from clifftop to sea level, and at its cul-de-sac end must be Shetland's smallest beach, say three feet by three feet. It is a place whose natural architecture recalls the dark salt-and-stone closes of oldest Lerwick and Stromness in Orkney, oldest thoroughfares of an all but extinct tribe of islanders who worked the sea in a small way for a living and a way of life.

But this sea alley of Nibon is a thoroughfare for skarfs. There is a nesting ledge high on one wall above that reverberating spot where the on-rushing sea gatecrashes the back-sliding retreat of the wave before. At this point, however, the alley is a few inches narrower than the shag's wingspan. The rock won't negotiate so the bird must. His homing flight alights on the sea just offshore and he swims up the alley, much as the old sea-booted Lerwick fisherman would have stamped up the flagstone closes. Where the man might have turned aside into a welcoming doorway and climbed a stone stair to house or alehouse, the skarf turns to face the rock and with a single all-but-vertical leap, crampons up the rockface on wingpoints to the nest.

What insights into the innermost workings of Shetland skarfs have won, what intimacies with the insides of islands! They go willingly in about the blackest, dripping-greenest holes and hell-holes of the wildest shores, nesting at times where no other eye of bird or fish or seal or man has ever blinked. How does the chick which first opens its eyes in these ancient recesses then respond to its first sight of the sun-bright ocean? The young of tern or oystercatcher, bonxie or diver, are spilled into the wide world almost from their first breath, but the young shag lives in a blackout for eight weeks, guessing at the world beyond, until the day it drops down the sea close, or swerves round the curve of a long sea cave to that world of winds and horizons and oceans and skies which is the Shetland the rest of us know. The skarf with its secret knowledge of Shetland has more right than most to the role of the islands' true bird symbol, but it would be too hard to turn such a bizarre physiognomy into a marketable commodity so Shetland advertises its wildness with the more photogenic crimson-throated diver sleekness or the cuddle factor of puffins.

Suddenly, from the highest point of the shore, the Drongs re-appeared, fantastical and gray and mysteriously enchanted by distance, bearded like every intervening headland by a white froth of sea. I found myself waving to them as I might wave to the far sighting of an instantly recognisable friend.

SANDWICK IS a small serration on the cutting edge of Shetland's sword blade, jutting farmland rooted in the sea. It is a place of dykes and dark earth crowned by steepening rough pasture where curlews assemble in loose spring choirs. Mostly, Shetlanders farm thoughtfully, and on a scale which recognises the scale of the landscape. Only in the valleys of Kergord and Tingwall are there hints of mainland farming techniques, exceptions to the prevailing philosophy of agriculture which more or less recognises nature as overlord. Robert Louis Stevenson was appalled by it, called it 'skimble-skamble', and doubtless when compared to the innovative landscape-staining farm techniques of the Lothians to which he would have been accustomed, Shetland's seemed a less than coherent land use. Yet he of all people might have been expected to recognise the worth of an agriculture which worked within the constraints of nature.

Doubtless he would have approved of Orkney, which by comparison is patchworked neater, tamer, the purpling of summer hills and moors a dwindling stain. The green march of new fields seems to be forever bullying the landscape to its will, redrafting it to new regimes, like the Vikings. Yet whether you hanker after islands dug and delved and draped in counterpanes, or obedient to nature's laws, it is a fact of life in these northlands that neither approach has staunched the flow of shed blood, the drift of islanders either from the outlying islands to the centre, or away from the islands altogether. There are many common bonds which bind Orkney and Shetland, but it is in the land and the way they use it that they pronounce their most marked distinctions. Orkney is somehow calmer, couthier, more at ease with itself. Shetland still wears wildness better even on its rarest, stillest, bluest day. It is a land in a perpetual crouch. Where is the next wind coming from?

Sandwick catches much of this. In its bay, its tight farms, its swooping headland, its small noosts where two-prowed boats (no blunt end) are hauled high, its tranquil Mousa Sound where you might expect an ocean's rage, its decrepit broch, its fractured coasts, its sweet and sour homes and landscapes...in all that there is a small encapsulation of all Shetland and the way it works its land. It is a worked-in, lived-in place, but it is wilder than it is worked-in and it is abandoned as much as it is lived-in. Up on the Ward of Burraland, the highest ground of Sandwick, the land is only roamed by sheep and whaups and winds. Out at No Ness, where outer and inner shore collide, it is roamed only by winds. It was there in a flattening wind from which the whole of Sandwick seemed to shrink, that I found a solitary goldcrest, battered and breathless and lost. We cowered in the lee of such shelter as we could find, eyeing each other, pondering our plights and puzzling each other's presence for an hour until, as evening grew, the wind suddenly fell away, the sea softened its shouting, and we each put a head above our chosen parapet. A warm calm drenched the headland and all Shetland seemed to sigh. The bird rose, curved away south-west, perhaps to work its way down the Shetland shore, to Fair Isle, to God knows where, a mite of grit in the eye of the wind, while I walked back up the headland towards the broch of Burraland, treading my shore in a daze, not daring to believe the calm, crouching like the land in the windlessness, wondering when and where and from what airt the next wind would hurry into this unlikeliest of nature's vacuums.

The calm held through the evening, and in its charmed embrace my mind danced away from Burraland across sounds and seas and eons, spinning such webs of unfettered imagination which are the products and the privilege of any mind washed up on such a shore on such an evening of almost festive stillness.

Burraland is a plundered place, a hint of a broch, a store of outlines and fragments, a green swelling on its headland through which the remnant stones protrude like a gray rash. It is impressive for all that, storing ironies and every broch's enigmas among the fragments. There on the hillside is the farmstead which was built with the broch's plundered stone, but the farmstead too is derelict, and like the broch, one more era's definition of domestic architecture which has been stranded and scrapped. I rummage through variations on that theme of the croft at Uyea built from the oldest rocks in Shetland, and the implications of such rocks for the inhabitants. How do these rocks of Burraland respond to re-employment 2,000 years after the shadowy broch people first heaved and hefted them? What rubs off? What unexplained incidents and episodes baffled

the crofters which the ingenious broch-builders might easily have explained away? When the crofters reordered those stones and capped them with slate, did they also build unwitting accommodation for the ghosts of the broch folk, and were their dreams of quietest waking hours disturbed with the incomprehensible conversations of lost tongues?

Perhaps those conversations dwelt on the merits of single-storey life in rectangular walls as against all that they knew of a home seven or eight storeys high where every wall was round. If there had been a listening ear among the Burraland crofters we might know more now about the brochs, about who built them, and why. Perhaps the ghosts of the Burraland broch still huddle on the hillside croft, and in that uncannily still evening light with the moon heaving low above the horizon, the keel of a dream might ground in the shallows of Sandwick.

> My spoor is marked
> where the white sands
> of time and dark tide
> coincide.
> Looking back
> down the moon-furrow
> of that northland night
> I sight
> a dwindling
> moon shadowing, sun-shunning race,
> whose shiftless, shifting sod
> I trod.
> Moon-painted men
> of primeval rite berthed here:
> foe-hunted, time-hounded
> they grounded
> uncanny craft. In these
> they dared the salt jaw
> till this their southland
> this sand
> gave brief but blessed
> shelter from the north-storms
> of their race.
> I trace
> now their fugitive landfall
> across this old, old shore;

soft footfalls match me stride
for stride.

But where I ache for words
from posterity's pursed lips
only tongues of salt and wrack
speak back.

By dawn my spoor
is scented, sifted, drifted by
the following hounds of the hunting tide;
they guide

still as they led the painted race
to their tryst with the moon place.

The sadness of Burraland is that its demolition created a house which was occupied for no more than, say, 200 years, while the broch itself might have been occupied for at least 1,000 years and stood as its own uninhabited monument for at least 1,000 years more. The sadness is compounded by the most pointed reminder a mile away across the sound to what has been, for there in all its miraculously intact glory is Shetland's showpiece of Iron Age architecture, the broch of Mousa.

Burraland and Mousa sit like gateposts on either side of Mousa Sound, and again, as you sit on the rocks beneath Burraland and above the sea, your thoughts are compelled back. Do you sit here on a wavelength of 2,000-year-old communications? Surely the mutual interests of the broch dwellers required some system of contact, even if it was only to signal the approach of a common enemy, for whatever else lay behind the unique structure and architectural principles of the brochs, there is no mistaking their defensive supremacy. Stewart Cruden articulates that supremacy in his book *The Scottish Castle*:

'...they would present to an enemy an impregnable front of solid high look-out and fighting position...' (although Cruden points out later that 'no weapons of war are found among broch relics, only implements of domesticity') '...and at this height the incoming arrow or sling-stone would be rapidly losing power. The immense thickness of the wall rendered them safe from undermining. No fire could drive the inhabitants out. The vulnerability of the entrance was reduced to a minimum. The only access was through a passage, long, narrow and low, leading to the courtyard space. Some halfway along it, checks or jambs were provided against which a heavy door (probably a stone slab) could be placed and barred....'

There are so many enigmas to the brochs, not the least of which is who built them. What civilised mind pondered and laboured over such problems as demanded the brochs for a solution? How was such a design arrived at, for the most astounding thing

of all about the brochs was they had no evolution and no prototype? They appeared only in perfect development, hundreds in the northern and western isles and the north of Scotland, a few scattered isolationists further south, but nowhere outside Scotland. Cruden writes: 'The mystery of their origin and of the people by whom they were made and occupied, and against whom they were intended, add greatly to the interest which they possess as early architectural works of outstanding merit. The origin of the style is wholly constructional, and the style so arresting as to imply a preconceived notion. It was an idea before it was a fact – the idea of a highly original mind.'

The benevolence of the fates has thrown its own protective cordon around the uninhabited island of Mousa, and enshrined on a shelf above the sea the bluntly towering gray thrust of Mousa broch. There is a ruined farm here too, but it was easier to gather building stone from the shore than dismantle the broch. Somehow, though, Mousa broch is diminished by its new role of tourist whistlestop, and I find its enigmas best served by the distance and the dignified landscape setting which the Burraland shore offers. It is only now that it has finally been overwhelmed in invasion, for its masonry has been commandeered by a colony of storm petrels. The fact that their instinctive nesting preference for burrows in steep boulderfields or ragged cliffs could be satisfied here is both tribute to a brilliant adaptation of nature and to the extent to which nature guided the hand of the broch builders. If, as Stewart Cruden claims, the broch is 'the most remarkable ancient castle of Europe', then Mousa is the most remarkable of that remarkable species.

It is a reasonable enough assumption that St. Ninian's Isle across the southern Shetland mainland was a broch site too, but such are the whims of time and tide and chance and storm on shores like these that while Burraland and Mousa linger on in their relative stages of survival, all anyone can say about St. Ninian's Isle with some confidence is that there was a settlement there between the 3rd and 1st centuries BC. So it was inhabited when the broch builders were at the height of their powers, and as likely to be home to the broch folk as not. Like Jarlshof, the same stones were reworked several times.

You can almost hear some Pictish council pronounce:

'Away with this old broch, what need have we to defend ourselves now that we are Christians? Let us build a church!'

How were they to know that the Vikings were in history's offing? If only the brochs had survived a few centuries more, even as habitable last resorts, how different the history of Shetland – and Orkney – might look to us now, for the Vikings would have found them no more penetrable than anyone else.

But it was the Picts who would immortalise St. Ninian's Isle for the prying eyes of eras like ours. Somewhere around 800 AD, and doubtless with the Vikings trampling about these shores, they stored away a small hoard of silver treasure here. The Vikings missed it, and so did the builders of two churches, the last a medieval one, the ruins of which still stubbornly thole the wind, the blown sand, the archaeologists, the traipsing tourists and the rabbits. But in 1955, a now famous excavation began to rummage down among the low, fat walls, and three years later, unearthed what is now known as the St. Ninian's Isle Treasure, the hoard of Pictish relics, much of it silver - bowls, brooches, spoons and other implements, sword hilts, chapes from sword scabbards, combs, and the jawbone of a porpoise.

There are clues about the treasure, but not many. The official HMSO booklet points out that one chape bears Latin inscriptions, 'on one side INNOMINEDS, that is "in nomine d(ei) s(ummi)", "in the name of God the highest", and on the other side RESADFILISPUSSCIO. The translation of this is a little more difficult, but it appears to say "Resad son of Spusscio", in which case Resad and Spusscio are two Pictish names and Resad was the owner of the sword scabbard.'

Or perhaps he was the silversmith who took it upon himself as he saw the longship prows round Burra to save his best work from the predatory eye of the invader, but lingered too long as he signed the hoard with the inscription on the chape.

Their longships cleave
these tremulous islands
scattering our histories
to our many winds
as if we had never been
re-writing all
as braggart sagas.

South! South! they cleave.
We are sheep
to their wolving,
peacemongers
to their warring.
If only our forefathers
had lingered longer
in the safe circle
of the broch. From there
we'd have bartered
a better peace.

Now the crimson
of my veins
must guard the silver

of my art. This treasury
must outlive the war.
It is a hint
I hide, pointing out
our lives to others,
peacemongers coming curiously
in their time.

I Resad, son of Spusscio,
carve and curve last words
on this small sword piece
'...INNOMINE...'
(that bellow at the door
is no fraternal Christian!
They are here too soon!
Quick...the box! The marker stone!
...the altar overwhelmed,
the stench of fresh flame)

'DS...'

Unspared, I fall
on my hoard. Skull of Resad
stand guard,
for my spilled blood
is warm, but cooling.

St. Ninian, hear me.

So it should not be hard to marvel at the dull gleam of old silver in Lerwick's museum, but they are fakes. The real ones were thought suitably important for the National Museum of Antiquities in Edinburgh, Shetland thought suitably unimportant that it could make do with copies. That rankles, with shades of Viking plunder. Indeed, for all the nationalistic affection with which Shetland has accorded Scotland, it would perhaps have been as well if the Vikings had found the St. Ninian's Isle Treasure. The Vikings had craftsmen enough at least to appreciate the treasure's worth, and might well have spared them. Shetland would at least have been spared a gift of fakes. It is an exclusively Shetland heritage which Professor O'Dell and his Aberdeen University team unearthed in 1958, and there is no reason why it should ever lie anywhere else.

Meanwhile, St. Ninian's Chapel has a nasty wire fence, a delapidated information board and the old graveyard is interred itself under years of blown sand and overwhelmed by unrelenting indifference. Who cares? Perhaps if Scott had 'discovered' the chapel as well as Jarlshof, it might have all been different. Whatever his worth as a writer (and I find him an unpalatable dust) he had an uncanny appreciation of the worth of symbolic artefact to the collective consciousness of a people, and power of persuasion enough to put the Scottish Regalia back on show in Edinburgh Castle, and retrieve the canon Mons Meg from languishing exile in the south. If he had unearthed the Picts' silver, or somehow got to hear of it, Shetlanders might still have the real thing to marvel at and inspire their lives.

Yet nature, at least, seems to care. It has conferred on the sacred island a land bridge of unique and exquisite sand architecture. This tombolo is a symptom of what geologists call a drowned coast (a strange terminology - surely the coast is always the last bit of land which the sea has yet to drown, but logic was never geologists' strong point and geology never mine). It is the work of the sea nagging away like a foul-mouthed tongue at faults in the coastal rock. Onto a wave-cut platform of rock the rising sea drags sediment and gravel and pebbles and sand, and lays down a natural causeway to islands like St. Ninian's or Fora Ness in Delting or a bay-bar across the end of a voe. Fora Ness has tombolo, bay-bar and mid-bay-bar, a complexity of land and water forms to delight the geologist and dazzle the eye of the landscape watcher.

Often the sea is trapped behind a bay-bar, and in time a new fresh water loch is born. Sometimes the light catches obliquely on the sea's underwater workings on the rock and sand underworld, and a voe wends away from you to the sea through bands of fleeting colour. Such a phenomenon is usually encountered on a bright gray day when land and sky are as colourless as cellophane. It was Laxo Voe I first met in such a mood, striped orange, purple, green, blue, gray, an aurora borealis of the ocean, constantly shifting, constantly shading, a restless, irresistible landscape.

Common terns huddled on the spit of shingle at the head of the voe, the wind plucking and puckering their feathers, ruffling their sleekit calm. They stood or sat, nebs-to-the-wind, in such a striking resemblance to a familiar painting by the greatest of all bird artists, Charles Tunnicliffe, that I inwardly applauded his powers as a naturalist as well as his art. A few weeks later I could compare the notes and the mental picture I had brought home with a copy of the painting, and renewed the applause. The painting ripples with movement - of brisk wavelets, of the bubbled and blown spume which trims the shore in a creamy lace, of breast and wing feathers and restless tails. Two of the birds are inflated like ruffs, the precise thought which lodged in my mind and in my pocket tape recorder on Laxo Voe. The three foremost birds point directly into the wind, and suffer less feather

ruffling than the second row of four birds. Three of the second row have heads turned at a small angle to the wind and there is more marked chaos among their feathers. You learn from a Tunnicliffe flock not to think of a species but of individual birds, and you learn to think of how a bird behaves. His terns, like mine on Laxo Voe, are purposely aligned to present the smallest possible feather surface to the wind. The spaces between the birds let the wind through, like a mesh. The effect of birds and wind and water and spit of land and light go beyond the sum of those parts, however, for they portray the birds in their landscape and that is the work of art.

Tunnicliffe once wrote: 'It is with the creation of a very different kind of beauty that this book will try to deal, that of line and form and colour on paper or canvas; a work of art in fact which, we hope, will have its own particular claim to be beautiful, not because it has slavishly imitated the form and colour of the bird but because it has used the bird and controlled it to create a new beauty.' There are many ways to watch birds in a place like Shetland, everything from the twitcher's frantic one-upmanship, to the lingering appraisal of a familiar bird in its landscape. That day on Laxo Voe was one in which I fancy a Tunnicliffe would have delighted.

The terns of Laxo Voe wrecked my fantasy-in-art then by rising as one bird, holding a low formation over the colour-play of the voe's waters, then suddenly they split, a starburst of birds. The effect was to watch the opposite in nature of a kaleidoscope, in which all the moving pattern-making pieces are white and the background vividly coloured. A solitary whimbrel, which the Shetlanders tellingly call 'peerie whaup' - little curlew - added a drab accessory to all these moving parts and their landscape. The memory I hold of that small moment in the eons of all Shetland's landscapes and all its birds has its 'own particular claim to be beautiful'.

Back at St. Ninian's Isle, the sea ranges through its more conventional colours - colourless and clear as glass in the sandy shallows, purpling over patches of seaweed, then the classic blue-green of all our northern and western isles. The brushstrokes of sand and sea here might just as easily be Iona as Shetland. Further out, beyond Bigton Wick, where the ocean proper sets in, the sea darkens and grays to a firm dark line. Out in the mouth of the wick, a single wave breaks hugely again and again, fully half a mile from any shore, collapsing not onto rock or sand or shingle but into its own chaotic whirlpool, like the sinking tail which signs off the whale's leap. Minutes of calm follow the convulsion, then the sea is seized again and the same one-wave maelstrom heaves itself into a new spasm. At the high point of each new wave, just as the top of it has caved in, a burnished and glowing turquoise curve catches the sun. It is the most brilliant and fragile shade, the nearest thing I have ever seen to that turquoise fire of the kingfisher which no painting and no photograph has ever ensnared. You artists who still hanker after that elusive shade, go to Bigton Wick on a day of fitful sun and fast winds and watch for the wave which breaks alone.

Shetland's colours are forever confounding artists (we can't all be Tunnicliffes). Here is an evening, for example, on the shore at West Sandwick on Yell, the light lying a-dazzle on the sea, as the sun dips towards the north-west. Beyond the spear of the sun a series of white lines seems to mark the surface of the water's pervasive gray-white, and give it the air of a lightly creased cloth. Far out, a lobster boat butts through the cloth and seals its own incision behind it, a new stitch to the tapestry which clothes all landscapes and to which we all respond in our ways:

Lowland Farmer

A cloud of rooks
darkens my sky
with its shaggy black weave;
the lured starlings, jackdaws
and lolling gulls
hang on the sheen
of their tumbling coat tails
and thread that coarse weave
with their own artless finery.
I frame their tapestry
to hang on the wide wall of my field.

Shetland Fisherman

A cloud of terns
pales my sky
with its white weave of snow
while far gannets
- a heavier weave of hailstones -
gash the sea's creased cloth
with honed needles.
I frame their tapestry
to hang on the waving wall of my sea.

Highland Climber

A pair of eagles
dusts my sky
with a stupendous weave;

the falcon rises to challenge
two Goliaths, fails and falls
from their dismissive grace
with a fast and vanquished swerve.
I hang no tapestries on mountain walls.
I kneel, I whisper to the Weaver.

It will always be easier for the poet than the painter in such a landscape. Here is a fulmar flying south down that Yell shore in that show of bravado and curiosity with which he greets all strangers on all shores. But as he flies, his starboard flank is on fire, a burning pink in the full glow of the evening sun. His port flank is gray and white, dulled by the shadow of his own flight. Now paint that, a fulmar half pink, half gray and white, the join a clearly discernible line down beak and head and spine, and who'll believe you ever saw such a thing? The more you wander the wild world, the more you marvel at its Tunnicliffes.

YELL, Eric Linklater once wrote, is 'the problem child of the archipelago'. It lies at a remove from the mainland hub of Shetland, but because it also lies at a remove from the outer islands of Unst (of the Hermaness showstoppers) and Fetlar (of the superstar snowy owls) and has no real ocean horizons, many travellers consign it to the oblivion of a stepping stone. It also suffered – and this was Linklater's point – from a depopulating drift. Just as London drains Britain, he argued, Lerwick drains Shetland. Yell being a seven-minute ferry ride from the Shetland mainland, Lerwick drained Yell quicker than most, and by 1962 so much of the lifeblood of Yell had drained away that the survivors convened a conference to discuss its plight. One recommendation of a subsequent report argued for the creation of a new centre of population in the north of Shetland, preferably on Yell, and another in the west. The most cursory glance around the Yell of today shows that precious little has changed for the better, and although on the mainland Bray burgeoned a little with the development of Sullom Voe, it is not a flattering tribute to that 30-year-old vision.

Yet for all that has drained away from Yell, it maintains a calm self-containment. As so often with stepping stone places, there are discreet and quietly hoarded treasures which you step on or miss completely as you press on to further shores. The pause, if you bother to make it, has rewards enough, if you can be bothered to prise them out. Yell is a small Shetland within Shetland, samples of all Shetland's tastes (bar the rarefied savours of Foula or Out Skerries), but more than samples, too – that 'enough' which is as good as the feast. My first tasting of Shetland savoured Yell with the most ardent relish, so that on my second visit, I set out my solitary writer's stall a dozen yards above the high tide on Mid Yell Voe at the island's waist. When we finally parted company, I had grown confident that here of all Shetland was the island where I would most cheerfully drop anchor, and haul up my nomadic instincts on noosts of contentment.

From my writing window, the voe double-bends away east like an 's' viewed from the bottom up where the sea has insisted on passage between the Head of Hevdagarth and the Hill of Lussetter. The head of the voe is a snug bay round a third bend over my right shoulder. Mid Yell is a voe which works for a living, its innermost shore well peopled in a loose coalition of ill-defined ragged-edged townships where narrow roads and tight corners are often rendered narrower and tighter by ad-hoc hospices of rotting, wrecked and dismembered vehicles. In many places, such heaped variations on a theme of rust offend visitors' sensibilities, mine among them. Here, where they are unabashedly gathered about the houses like grotesque garden gnomes, they seem much more a part of the landscape, not a pretty part of it, but a component which the landscape has somehow accommodated.

These townships - Stevenson's 'skimble-skamble' invention seems somehow more appropriate here - work the land and the sea in a small way, piecemeal versatilities of crofting, fishing, a fish farm, and as much tourism as cares to drop by, which is not a lot. There are birdwatchers on the Yell ferry but they are hell-bent on Fetlar where with luck they will see a far white blur, a snowy owl sitting on the moor like a milestone. If they have time, they will hurtle through Unst for a glimpse of the ageing albatross which regally camps among the Hermaness gannets. At Mid Yell, my wildlife companions are humbler, less exotic, more reliable, and ever present. A finger of rock uncovers with the ebb, the sea unfurling back from the bottom of the garden. It is commandeered at once by a pair of maalies (the Shetlandic names work better here, ring truer, or is that just the fanciful conclusion of an outsider's ear which divines more native voices here than elsewhere in Shetland). I have already become accustomed to the maalies' voices harping on and on at each other through every waking hour, half the sleeping ones and indecently early dawns. Here they sit and sun themselves, court and mate and chatter and fend off more or less all-comers, but with varying degrees of energy and enthusiasm according to the nature of the intrusion. Other maalies may linger up to a point, but a ritualised bicker is just as likely to end in a threatening lunge, and the pecking order is restored. At low tide, though, with the rock fully uncovered, there is comfortable room for a dozen birds, guards are dropped, and tolerances grow generous.

The dunters like the rocks too, and a pair from the voe's semi-permanent floating population parade ashore in clockwork jerks, then fold themselves roundly into that pebbly posture of repose which looks the most delectably natural attitude in the seabird kingdom. It is a sumptuous pillow on which an eider sleeps when it lays its head deep into the plumage of its own back. On a warm spring day with all that season's promise, what warmer contentment can there be? Perhaps the maalies have a sense of aesthetics, and permit the dunters for their therapeutic ornamental value? A grounded squadron of spring-lingering turnstones come prodding and wrack-stabbing and are commanded to keep their distance from the maalies. This they do. It would not be much of a contest. The garden's residents, Shetland's very own sub-species of starling and wren, busy themselves obliviously about the maalies' couch and pour much scorn at their heads from the nearest fencepost. Shetland starlings have an impressive repertoire of mimicry. The garden male does a bewilderingly convincing curlew, lapwing, redshank and gull mew, as well as all his own muttering and screeching virtuosity. The wrens prospect under the unfamiliar shadow of my car, up onto the front axles. A nesting site? This, remember, is a place where a car can rest immobile for a very long time, and certainly become part of a wren's landscape after a season or two. The car is rejected, probably because, having not yet lost a bonnet or a wing, it is too dark. Also, it wasn't here last week. Small wings blur on. The maalies watch and wonder at the blur. What can be the point in such impatient industry?

Then a wide, bubbling wake approaches from the sea, a gray head surfaces, and all birds defer. When an otter pauses on the rocks, no bird should be seen dead there. The otter sniffs, stands, turns, rejoins the sea, leaving me to wonder if the whole thing actually happened. The maalies are the first birds to return. Two heedie maas - black-headed gulls - and two swaabies stand in the shallows facing the shore like policemen patrolling a football match with their backs to the action.

Droves of the gull tribes loiter about the salmon cages of the fish farm and the wind is forever full of their cries and their drifting, dragging flights. Their voices, the bickering maalies, the fluting waders, the screaming chocolate-prowed heedie maas, the creamy ooze of the dunters, the reedy yelps of the shaldurs, the indescribable duet of the raingeese...that is the unorchestrated song of this shore.

On calmer days you see and hear the great fish thrash the water of their cages half a mile out into the voe, a raw show of energy, but it impresses in the way that tigers impress in a circus. The mind's eye sees the salmon of the ancient tribal stream and the ocean, and the mind simply gnaws at an unease. Henry Williamson wrote it with a wonderful simplicity: 'Salmon feed in the Atlantic and return to the freshwater rivers to spawn, and, by this arduous and pleasurable act, give of themselves to the immortality of salmon.' There is precious little immortality in a cage. There are jobs, however, and all the euphoria and the flaws of a boom industry which has stopped booming. The boats trundle out and back wearing the same groove down and up the voe and in every weather and wind, and even round the 's' bends of the voe it can blow hard enough for the waves to obliterate sight and sound of the boat. The business of feeding and fattening and killing cannot afford to be any respecter of tides. The new corrugated shapes above the Mid Yell pier are the business end of the fish farm, where the immortality of salmon is packed and coloured and canned, and offers the islanders a precarious source of the lifeblood of employment. In a Shetland so pock-marked with the derelict headstones of extinct communities, it is hard to deny any community's eager clutch at any new source of lifeblood. Yet the unease which many feel about fish farming is here too, and not just among incomers, conservationists and tourists who don't like the look of the cages. I plead for a more thoughtful way of wresting a living for such places than the quick overkill fad industries which now exploit so many of our isolated land- and sea-scapes. I have no fast cure-all, of course, and my pleading will not fill Shetland's bellies and bank accounts, but I cannot believe enough people, either in small communities or in government, are working together to try to find a better way.

Mid Yell's fish farm is on a reasonable scale, the cages innocuous enough and the shore buildings no worse than many a modern building in Shetland, although that is no great compliment. (The fad industry psychology again...consider the architecture of fish farms then consider the stone skills of the lodberry builders; a trite comparison perhaps, but there is an impatience about the fad industries and an unwillingness to make long-term commitments which is at odds with islands' rootedness in the sea.)

A squall hammers across the voe. The boat working out at the cages dances to its tune. The cages' platforms become a chancy walkway. The boat hauls in another netful (the net not trawled but suspended from the boat's own derrick) of salmon whose brief lives are short on immortality. But still the fish must be harvested, and in Shetland at least, even harvesting from a fish farm demands skills with a small boat in big weather, a contempt for discomfort, and risk. That much at least is unchanged since Peter was a fisherman.

The boat backs off from the cages into another blast. The squalls have slowly caught up with each other and begun to mount a day-long storm, gale driven and rain-drenched. But this is a killing day and there are jobs to be done. Gulls in their reinforced hundreds hurtle down from every compass point, dozens scrabble madly at every discarded fragment of fish. Only a handful of the mob will catch so much as a morsel, and as with the terns of Nibon there are always bonxies patrolling the flock, eager to make an offer a successful gull cannot refuse. Between boat trips, the gulls subside down onto the croft fields beyond my window where the starlings and shaldurs run the gauntlet of their oaths. Through

the height of the storm, only the eiders cling to the water, riding its peaks and troughs, flexing their wings, the drakes jerkily displaying, parodies of every bathtub toy duck you ever saw.

All week and every day, I have watched the crofter across the voe in about his sheep. It is a big field by Mid Yell standards, bounding down the steep flank of the voe like a dry ski slope with a shelf in the middle. The sheep are lambing, and every day man and dog arrive by Land-Rover at the top of the field and trudge down it. From this distance, of perhaps three-quarters of a mile, the man looks tall and springily-striding, the dog low and watchful and wide-running to the manner born. Today, on the day of the big storm, the man appears clad head-to-toe in the brightest orange oilskins you ever saw. The only brighter shade in Shetland lights the night sky above Sullom Voe. I watch the boat battle back from the cages. I watch the crofter's orangey stride back up his hillside. I watch my window rattle in its frame. I think of all the Shetlanders who ever cast off in a small boat or bent their back to till an unwilling piece of land. It doesn't matter what you do here, how carefully you lay your plans, you can never batten down nature, and there is no enterprise, no matter how fleeting or how traditional, which does not flourish or fail at her whim.

NESS OF GALTAGARTH is a small, flat and infertile island, umbilically threaded to Yell by its tombolo sand bar, and, if you are given to judging sausages by their skins, it looks boring. But I love sausages, whatever their skins, and I tramped out the sand bar across a small swathe of one of Shetland's many Hamna Voes (the name simply means a voe with a harbour, and crops up anywhere which offers boats a fair shelter) with expectations high. There is no corner of a landscape like Shetland which declines to unearth small treasures for the mind hell-bent on the joy of discovery.

The presence of what I took to be a caravanette parked out on the island beyond the end of the sand bar promised convivial company (it is not a beach-loafer's island, but not much of Shetland is). An artist? Another writer? A fellow wanderer of the wilds? A naturalist? All these things rolled into one enigmatic wilderness genius? It was not until I saw the passenger door wilting against one wheel that I paid the vehicle closer attention and had my joy-fires of discovery dampened by one more of Shetland's wrecks. The van bore the legend of its working life on the seaward flank, as tell-tale as a boxer's broken nose, these words in bold capitals: 'FISH AND CHIPS'. It is less than likely that such a business made much of a living on Yell, so I wonder how far the van had been driven or towed to die here? It seemed a lot of trouble to go to, particularly as the owner could hardly be expected to escape detection. There aren't that many fish and chip businesses in Shetland, and such a conspicuous vehicle in such a conspicuous place suggests the absence of fear of prosecution. Surely it irks every passer-by on the road between Burravoe and the ferry? But there is much about Shetland's attitude towards wrecked vehicles which passes understanding.

The island's seaward shore is a treachery of round and knife-edge boulders and wet seaweed spilling down from an eroding peat bank. The peat, where it contemplates the rock, overhangs or crumbles away into a more or less continuous alleyway, the width of an otter – which is not coincidence. Shetland is a benevolent host to otters. Hundreds of miles of untrampled coast, tidefuls of food and good shoreline cover provide otters with their best British stronghold. Ness of Galtagarth is as good as a broch for an otter's purposes, and I had been on the island less than half an hour when I saw head and tail cut the surface 50 yards offshore, swimming purposefully in that porpoising manner of an otter on the march. For as long as the shore permitted, I kept pace with the otter, running and scrambling while it was underwater, crouching and freezing when it surfaced. You can often come close enough to an otter homing in on the shore with this technique, especially on a bouldery shore like this. Once, on Sleat of South Skye, I watched an otter climb out of the sea into my camera viewfinder after I had plotted his crab-carrying course towards a flat rock, crouched close, and focused the camera. We were 15 yards apart when the otter landed, and at the first clatter of the camera shutter, it looked up and asked (a clearly interrogative inflexion): 'Haaah?'

I said: 'Haah!' and clattered some more pictures. He crunched on crabshell, then said: 'Haaaaah?' and stood up.

I said 'Haaaaah?' too, and on that basis we established a ten-minute conversation which was only interrupted while the otter went back to the sea twice to catch two more crabs. The otter has doubtless forgotten the moment, but I have not. Not in ten years.

But now my Shetland shore was curving away from the porpoising one as it held a course clear across Hamna Voe, and in my eye-straining search for a last head-and-tailing glimpse among the waves, I failed to see what I should have seen, and squandered what could prove to be the best opportunity to watch an otter that I will ever know. Instead, I became frantically aware of a second animal, a huge gingery dog otter, curled up and dozing in the sun just below the bank where I walked, and perhaps five paces away. I registered one burning image of the rhythmical heave of his flank before something in my startled silence gatecrashed the cordons of his sleep. He took the 20 yards of shoreline rocks at a flat-out blur, dived without pause into the water, and from that sanctuary, turned and scrutinised me in silent outrage. Then he dived and was gone. I considered his sprint, and the terrain it had covered. I equated it with me covering 100 metres of the Cuillin Ridge in ten seconds, from a sleeping start.

I wandered on along the shore, finding much evidence of otter presence but no more otters. Instead, there was a black rabbit and a dreary pair of whimbrels which shrieked dryly at me and stepped up from the shingle into the air, hung like coat-hangers for a moment and wheeled away across the voe. Walking back across the low crown of the island, the wind eased away and the sun burned fiercely through again. The next day I had to leave Yell, and it snowed.

Shetland thrives on such extremes. You pare away one more layer of the island fabric seeking enlightenment and understanding, and just when you think the place has spoken to you in words you can understand, it confronts you with the opposite, and demands that you try and make sense of that. In the same heady 24 hours of heatwave to snow, I relinquished my small and storm-bound writer's cell on Yell for a night in Busta House, high and handsome, opulent, tranquil and leafy. My Yell host's garden bore the modest fruits of her labourings against the snap of all manner of winds. She was an emigrant from Nottinghamshire 30 years ago, and among the wizened and tortured runts of trees with which she had stoically persevered were a handful which first rooted in Sherwood Forest where they had every right to anticipate a splendid and privileged existence. Instead they found their way to Shetland, and at 30, they were old and going nowhere, stung by salt rubbed into the wounds inflicted by so many winds. Yet at Busta House, no more than 15 miles and a ferry hop to the south-west, and seemingly enjoying no more and no less shelter than Mid Yell, it is the difference accorded by mature trees in a Shetland setting which dignifies the place. The house, too, is an exceptional building, in which the ambitions and egos of lairds of the 16th and 18th centuries have been tempered by stonemasons and architects who adhered to native traditions and proportions. So the wings of the house are tall and narrow and so are the windows; the slate roofs fit thoughtfully inside the gables to thwart winds; a small harbour and dovecote obey the same sense of place. Shetland's lairds' houses tend to be big and bold and blunt. Because Busta has trees, it is also beautiful.

It was there at Busta House, now a hotel, that I compared notes with Colin Baxter and his family (they arrived that day, a perilous one-wheeled landing at Tingwall as the ingenuity of Loganair's pilots was put through one more test, this time a particularly bilious species of crosswind). They were bound for a week on Foula where we would join forces again later in the week, and for a few hours before they flew on we prowled the high ground of Burra Isle where both the Clift Hills on the Shetland mainland and the hills of Foula glittered with the night's new snow. The light that morning was a jingling dance, the air a heady drink, the landscape with its sun and snow and sea colours and pale sand and blazing yellow lichens was living out one of those moments of all its times and tides which caught a glimpse of the unalloyed purity of nature. But the sun burned down and

the snow rolled up the hills like a blind and the wind hurtled back and the thing was done. Colin and family flew west and I drove east over the hill to Lerwick and the Sound-trampling ferry for Bressay.

BRESSAY IS another of those stepping-stone places where the stone-steppers miss the point. For most of its visitors it is a single-track road on the way to Noss, and while there is no denying the wonder and the scale and the raw energies and passions of that island's seabird cliffs, I would trade an hour out at the Loch of Grimsetter under the Ward of Bressay for a month on Noss. Grimsetter is elemental Shetland, possessed of that bitter-sweet sense of beauty which I recall from a distance as a lonely ache. The loch lies under the heathery slopes of the Ward, a sheet of slate, with lesser hills to the north and south. But the burn which drains it to the east becomes almost instantly a waterfall, and its fall is down a 100-foot cliff to the sea. Bonxies and kittiwakes flock here to bathe, and fulmars drift down in twos and threes. A pair of red-throated divers, inevitable badge of Shetland's moor lochs, wail and gargle and circle each other and wonder at the commotions of the kittiwakes. In early winter, with the hills stiffened by a week of frozen snows, a long triumphant skein of whooper swans droop brassily down out of the north sky. Hark the herald birds!

The single track across the moor to the Loch of Grimsetter is traipsed by many ghosts. All around Grimsetter's hill slopes stand the ruins of cleared townships. One house is occupied, but even that is so shrouded in lintel-high bushes that it is as blind to its landscape setting as the sightless door and window sockets of the ruins.

I made a high circuit of the loch, threading the ruins, admiring the craftsmanship of the thin, flagstone-like rock of the walls, dropping to the burn at the seaward edge, letting the clifftop dictate my course for an hour. Its first command was to divert round the flanks and the back of Millburn geo, an angular gouge into the rock of the island perhaps 200 feet deep, 50 yards wide, tapering towards the back, like a box canyon of ten-storey buildings. The top of the cliff is a scene of small slaughter, as though a miniature war game of the shore had been fought here, and moved on leaving the battlefield uncleared. Bits of birds, entrails, skulls, wings, even an intact skeleton of one of last year's chicks. It has all survived the gales of winter, and as Shetland's seabird tribes vie ever more desperately for the right to survive another nesting season in the face of increasingly insurmountable odds, doubtless the thin white line of clifftop slaughter will fatten through the summer, until one more winter's gale blasts through the jetsam.

The discovery of a dyke and ditch running steeply down to the loch shore sparks off a new impulse. By crawling or crouch-walking for about a quarter of a mile, I could reach the shore unobserved by the bustling bird life of the loch. In particular, I could come close to the red-throats and watch their pre-nesting cruise. So 15 minutes later I was precariously perched by the last yard of the dyke, one foot on a dry rock and one on a submerged one, the camera and the glasses well lodged in apertures of the dyke, the divers 50 yards away and closing, the fulmars dropping by in desultory visitations to inspect my cramp-inducing crouch, the kittiwakes bathing and cartwheeling far across the loch. The bonxies were at the far end of the loch, anything up to 30 at a time, and after bathing they drifted off to a small green knoll where they stood around and dried off like an inert blackcock lek. The divers were disappointingly placid, except that for a few minutes they swam close enough for the glasses to pick out every minute feathered contour of their exotic plumage, but thoughtful study was forever being compounded by the kittiwakes lifting off and dragging their cries through the background, and settling to bathe again. It is an extraordinary ritual, and although individual birds came and went, the flock as an entity kept up the process for all the hours that I wandered the loch and its hills. At its peak, the flock was 200 strong, and bathed in a long thin string of birds like an advancing army. The bathing itself is half a vigorous minute, then the whole flock rises, circles, settles, bathes again, each rising and falling set to the most expressive calling and crooning of all seabirds. I caught one pointed cameo in the glasses when the divers were no more than 30 yards away and facing me: as the kittiwakes rose particularly noisily behind them, they both spun in opposing circles to face the sound, and in the process their heads almost touched, presenting me with the pyjama-striped backs of their necks, then with the same precision of movement, they wheeled back to face me with their eyes of blood. They do nothing – except walk – without distinction.

South from the loch, the Bressay shore lowers and divides into a triumvirate of geos. One of these, a deep triangular wedge tapering down to the sea, contemplates high-rise Noss. Noss is spectacular from without. Bressay is beautiful from within.

There is a fourth aperture in this shore, a deep lagoon, a calm and narrow tongue of sea among low, slab-sided rocks. From high above that tranquil water, I saw a bull gray seal break the surface well inside the lagoon. I froze until he dived again, and believing I could work the same otter-stalking technique I used on Yell, charged down the bouldery shore while he was submerged, but I had failed to notice 12 boulder-coloured seals which had already hauled-up at the head of the lagoon, and now greeted my gatecrashing dash with a concerted and decisive panic. The slowest seal took three seconds to hit the water, and within ten seconds there were 13 heads contemplating my foolish stance, all of them gathered at the seaward end of the lagoon, 100 yards off. It is at a time like this that a solitary man acknowledges that he is a fish out of water when he tackles nature on his own terms. To see one seal and miss 12 nearer seals is an eloquent enough commentary on the blinkered nature of the human species. I became conscious as I tried to halt my charge that I was acting out the kind of role a cartoon animator might have devised for the ranger in Yogi Bear, and I found myself hoping fervently that I was not being watched. As far as I know, I was not, except by the seals, and they had doubtless assessed my character and my capabilities at first sight. I watched them dive and drift seaward, and slowly assembled a small plan to repair the damage.

I walked purposefully away from the lagoon until I was out of sight of its water, then doubled back to the lee of its highest flanking rocks. I inched an eye over the seaward edge to find the seals milling at the edge of the lagoon, and one emboldened female beginning to swim tentatively back through the lagoon itself. She surfaced and paused and turned, but turned again, and dallied uncertainly. I now crawled and slid over ledges and slabs until a small gully offered a hidden descent right to the lagoon's edge, and no more than a dozen yards from where the seals had been lying. There I could take up a crouching stance where no seal could see me until it had swum past, and with the wind and my stillness working for me, I would wait and see what happened. I primed the camera and waited. It took 20 muscle-aching minutes, and when the first seal reappeared I was handed one more salutory rebuke, for she came not from the sea but the shore. She had obviously swum back in while I was negotiating the slabs and hauled-out directly beneath me, where I couldn't see her! Now she was staring up the lens of my camera from a dozen feet away, an entrancing cat-faced creature with eyes of black silk and the sunlight reflected from the water dancing a small polka across her brow. My hand went cold on the camera, I heard my heart thud. It is an unfailing, exultant response to being one-to-one with nature at closest quarters. There is a primitive excitement about such moments, especially when you have worked to achieve them, and no amount of the encountering diminishes the excitement or tames the awe. I rage at all those exquisitely filmed TV wildlife documentaries which trivialise the images of nature with the most bland of spoken commentaries by professional voices. I want to know what the cameraman felt and thought. I want to feel his hands go cold, hear his heart thud. The professional voice may be slick production, but it is a lie and it denies nature her true impact.

I bring a marginally more confident camera technique to such encounters these days. Colin is generous with advice when we work together and I have learned a little. I have seen him stalk a landscape where I might stalk a seal, heard the exultation as the perfect stalk bears fruit. Now my own stalked quarry poses, still as a landscape, and the first three shots only fired her curiosity so that she

swam closer. The fourth unnerved her, however, or perhaps she made some sense of my crouching stillness. She fled. I risked a leg movement, but my foot was halfway between its old niche and an exploratory grasp on a new one when the head of the big bull reversed into sight, eyes closed, nose up. He 'stood' on end sunning himself, and was oblivious to my presence. Clearly nothing of the female's alarm had transmitted itself, or perhaps bull seals are above receiving messages from such waifs. This one certainly wore an omnipotence about his jowls. I returned my foot to its old niche on the devil-you-know basis, and the old ache crept back into my leg. The bull seemed as deaf as he was indifferent, quite unresponsive to the camera shutter. He bared four chins, a prodigious hint of the 600lbs of body weight which he now contrived to manoeuvre like a cork. Occasionally his eyes drooped open, his nostril flared, a chin crinkled. Then his head righted itself - eyes front - and he tilted for the sea throwing me a glimpse of the back of his neck, half a yard wide, as he dived.

He was replaced almost at once by a new female, swimming on the surface with her head and tail submerged so that only her back and flanks were out of the water, like Orkney. Over the next hour, several seals swam past and lingered, but they all remained in the water, doubtless still unnerved by my rude interruption of their afternoon's peace, perhaps still sensing or resenting something of my presence. At their apparent reluctance to haul out and relax I finally hauled out myself and ate a lunch high above the storm beach. From that distant outpost, I saw the seals swim right up the lagoon to the shore, and by the time I had begun to climb the Ward, half of them were back on their rocks, drinking sun. So I walked conspicuously away, lured up the flanks of the Ward of Bressay by the beckoning cries of snipe and golden plover, the moor song which mingles so sweetly with the shore's chants - the dunters, rippacks, shaldurs, bonxies, aalins, swaabies, and heedie maas. I was becoming fluent.

The Ward of Bressay is a cornerstone of Shetland, a crow's nest from which to spy out land and sea, but it is a dirge of a climb up the road on its north slope and a toilsome plod through the heather above Bressay's east shore. The summit is a clutter of dishes and masts and huts, too, and the highest slopes are slashed with peat workings and pock-marked with more wrecked cars. But if you can shutter your mind to all that, raise your eyes instead to Yell, Unst, Fetlar, Out Skerries, Whalsay, up and down the Shetland mainland from Ronas Hill to Sumburgh Head. At your feet is the sea traffic of the Sound, the spreadeagle of Lerwick on its hill, and a crackling tinfoil sea that glitters away south to Fair Isle and the rest of the world. I fancy there is no five-minute boat ride in the land which unlocks such a hoard of differences as the flat-out ferry from tousled Lerwick to Bressay the beautiful.

Chapter Four

THE LAND WITHIN

THE SEA taints every shade and savour of the Shetland landscape. It is hard to get four miles from the sea, harder still to feel land-locked or rooted in anything other than a fragment of the seabed which the oceans have simply offered up on a short-term lease.

There is a land within, however, a spasmodic landscape of short valleys and high lochan-strewn moors. Occasionally you stumble on a small river, with the startling recognition that it has been a long time since you stumbled on a river. The Burn of Roerwater is the principal artery of that swack of moorland north of Ronas Voe which culminates in the thrust of Ronas Hill, the summit of all Shetland; at 1,475 feet it is all that is left of the mountain land that once was, all, that is, but skylined Foula which throws a mountainous aura across 14 miles of the ocean. The Burn of Roerwater drains a chain of lochs of which the three most prominent are Roer Water itself, Clubbi Shuns and Maadle Swankie. Just when you thought you were becoming fluent, too! Roer Water could be 'the reedy loch', Clubbi Shuns may or may not be 'the pool of the lumpy hill', and Maadle Swankie even eludes such straw-clutching as that. It is at this point, when you blunder in among the most ancient names amid the wildest of Shetland landscapes that you become painfully aware of that little learning which can be dangerous. Memorising a clutch of bird names doesn't make you a linguist.

This too is a bird place. The riverbank chirps with staneychaakers. All the way up the burn they stand pertly on their stanes and chaak, or dive vertically upwards to pluck a passing insect from its pilgrimage, or dash - a foolhardy venture - to flicker irritants in the face of cruising bonxies or prospecting merlins. I miss the dippers in places like this, and the herons, but neither of them finds favour in Shetland, and I must learn, as all travellers from the Scottish mainland must, that such similarities as I find with the hills and moors of home are only skin-deep. You must take Shetland as Shetland, not as an outpost of Scotland. It is as true of its social life and its culture as it is of dippers and herons. The very moors themselves teach you the same lesson, for of all Shetland's landscapes, theirs is the one which wears traces of familiarities, and no matter how much you feel you have acclimatised to Shetland the sea place, these folded away moors converse in familiar speech - the wheatears, the omnipresent larksong, the pibrochs of golden plover and curlew and the yelps of the big gulls. It is a mainlander's eye which scans all these and their heather-brown terrain. But pause and turn to follow the flight of an Arctic skua - no mainlander's flight that - or

to put sun or wind on your face, and you see a far voe where a tanker sails past a skerry, an immense intruder which jogs your mind back into that sea frame from which it had been dislodged by the moors' deception. Or a sudden rise in the ground on the moors of Yell throws you a glimpse of Ramna Stacks, distant and disjointed black shapes which (because a haze has blurred the shape of the sea) appear to float in a way which rock never does. But that is the sea side of the place, the island rootedness of where you stand, even when it is the moor's heartbeat you hear.

These moorland lochs like Roer Water and the hundred or so more which glitter across the northern Shetland mainland are the heartland of the red-throated divers. The sound and the sight of the divers in turn seem somehow to embody the spirit of the moors. It is something I have thought about often and find it difficult to articulate, and it has parallels in ospreys fishing a loch on Speyside or ptarmigan on a plateau boulderfield. It is a sense of a creature in its place, a perfect meshing of wildlife and wild landscape, an elemental appropriateness. It only occurs, to my mind at least, in a handful of landscapes and with a handful of creatures. I find it here now, with the divers of Roer Water. The moorland hags give good cover, and I find my diver pair far across the loch. I watch for half an hour to see if they will come closer but they are idly content with the wrong end of the loch. So I plot a route round the shore which I can achieve unseen, a murky crawl over heather and naked peat until I roll down a short bank to find the perfect couch with a sheltering rock and the divers drifting slowly towards me. Then one bird cries with that long dwindling wail of courtship, a note with ocean winds in it, an echo of an empty landscape, the hard-edged call of a bird unequivocally of the northlands.

The water sparkles suddenly as the sun begins to bully away the chilly smirr of the morning, but there is no warmth in the relentlessness of winds. The divers spin together through glints of vivid blue water, and the sun strikes the deep plush of their plumage, enriching the crimson throat, glittering in the matching eye, sleeking down the neck stripes. Again, their circling patterns like a slow, formal dance, create two delightful cameos of bird behaviour. Once as they swim away from each other in opposite directions their backs coincide in my sightline, and with their characteristically up-tilted heads, the silhouette of a Viking longboat briefly assembles. Once a lark starts singing suddenly and loudly in a corner of the shore; the divers, both facing me, turn to look at the source of the sound in perfect unison, over their left shoulders, and with the same precision swing back satisfied, as though the whole thing had been choreographed. And you thought people invented synchronised swimming!

A new intrusion blurs out from the shore, a white bird, diver sized, but looking much more of a duck. I puzzle over its shape and size and colouring for a few minutes (and the bobbing waves of the moorland wind make careful observation difficult) and eventually diagnose a long-tailed duck in winter plumage, and therefore without a long tail. The divers, which follow every sound and movement about the watersheet, first herd the duck into a corner, then with a clearly purposeful intent drive it out of their waterspace. It settles eventually, after a nervous circuit of the loch during which two bonxies, suitably invigorated by the duck flight, suddenly swirl down on the divers, but two vehement croaks rebuff them. Then one of them angles sharply away from the divers, makes a bee-line for my rock, brakes above my head like a landing gannet, and with an awesome gesture of wingpower, banks across my face and retreats, filling my mind with a thousand images of St. Kilda where I first ran a bonxie gauntlet. I have been warned.

The wind eases. The sun burns through. The divers yawn. The pace of life for the spirit of the moors is kind, at least for a slow afternoon before the tumult of the nesting season. The red-throated divers are back in their heartland and when they cry their ocean siren-song, the whole moor listens. I listen too, and revel in the magic of it all.

I eased away from the loch, throwing a wide diversion through the late afternoon and into the evening among the lochs of the north. There were three more pairs of divers, each pair inscribing calm circles on its own loch, and when I sat for half an evening hour on the Beorgs of Housetter high above the lochs, I threw the net of my mind on these waters, on the lochs of Yell and Unst, Fetlar and Foula and all their divers, and the significance of those landscapes for them. There are 700 pairs in Shetland, 70% of the British population, and they too are hampered by the sand eel controversy for they fly to and from the sea to feed. For the divers, 1988 was the worst season since monitoring started in 1980, and 1989 almost no better. For reasons which I am slow to admit to, for they hinge on the very human failing of holding favourites among nature's tribes, I grow angrier at the threat to the divers than to the other seabirds. It comes back to the sense in which they embody the spirit of the moors. If that spirit is taken from the moors, and if its absence is proved to be the result of an unjustifiable and unsustainable fisheries' policy, then Shetland itself will have driven out a crucial element of its own character, and one which it may find to be irreplaceable.

By mid evening, the smirr was settling down for the night, the winds were thudding across the high bouldery acres of the Beorgs of Housetter where the standing stones have long since given up the unequal struggle and lain down. A golden plover spilled its display song high above, a golden smirr of notes which drenched the old stones like a coating of lichen, followed by staccato calls with a sudden slow pump-action flight during which the bird all but stalls. It is the last voice of the day, the gold and the stalling alternating, a high and bewitching aerial ballet of which I never tire. Cloud spilled wearily down the flanks of Ronas Hill and the long spring evening tired of itself early. Last night it was still light at midnight. Tonight it is dark by 10.30. All over Shetland, 700 pairs of red-throated divers roost darkly, shrouded by incomprehension. How do you explain the actions of its fellow Shetlanders to a raingoose?

THE MOORS of north Yell are bisected by an old unmetalled road, not so much a road as two furrows of bare earth and stone. The moor grasses and heathers grow thickly up the centre, and only the tread of an occasional passing Land-Rover (say one a week) keeps the moor's territorial ambitions in check. On a vigorous billowy day when the sky is so vast that you can fear for the perilously small fragment of your island in that greater scheme of elemental things, the road makes for delectable walking. It glitters as you walk, almost as if it has been sprinkled with broken glass, but it is only the sun flinting among the stone. For all that June beckons a week away, the moor is still a winter-shaded brown. Spring takes a little longer to make its point hereabouts. The only challenge to that monochromatic colouring is the sky-blue sheen of two lochans where they lie like place mats on the moor's spread cloth. On a higher slope, six crofts stand in a spacious huddle, hoarding their own shadows away from the sun. There a new fence holds back the moor, but it has done nothing to hold back the march of people away from the place. The usurping sheep graze and green the land right up to the brown moor's edge.

The track is a mile into the moor when you stumble across what could be a quirky piece of bureaucratic Shetland humour. A small crescent has been stolen from the moor, and a newly painted sign on a new concrete post proclaims 'Passing Place'. There are others – perhaps four in three miles – and the next one is thoughtfully placed on the skyline about half a mile away so that on those few days a year when the high moors are not locked away in their own dreich screens of mist or worse, passing Land-Rovers can deliberate on who has the right of way at a distance of half a mile. I wonder how long the road was a road before someone found it necessary - or, as I still suspect, funny - to give it passing places.

As you climb (the road rises to about 300 feet), the moor unfolds, unveils more lochs and lochans, and far horizons assemble. Ronas Hill, again, inevitable, rears beyond the Sound, headlands and stacks emerge miles off, so that the moor appears to wear a bizarre frieze at its outermost edge. Plunge into the moor from the summit of the track and find a landscape so unexpectedly flat that its lochans look as if they are about to spill over the brim of the land. The map represents this landscape as a gathering of blue tadpoles joined by their tails. Such is the swarm of lochans and small burns on moors like these that most of them are anonymous.

The peat hags, often head high, look dead, still places at first glance. Yet a lingering second glance unearths the spoors and traces of teeming lives. Hare and otter tracks punctuate the traceries of wandering sheep, and the webbed feet of bonxies and gulls are everywhere. You might find a thin line of stoat tracks too, or the purposeful twiggy tread of the wader tribes. The sudden appearance of two oystercatchers plowtering through a hag, and the vivid patterns of their plumage in flight make you realise how little of pattern and definition there is to the Shetland moors. So often when I walk among them I think of them as a reservoir of nature's superglue, binding and bonding the Shetland landscape, a hidden inner strength at the heart of the islands. I have made a big circuit of half a dozen high lochs around Kussa Waters, dreaming with the moorland birds as they whoop and wander through their spring rediscoveries of old haunts and rituals. I make it something of a ritual too, to go among the high-moored, dome-skied places of the land with the spring birds, for their energy and their passion and their commitment is a benevolent and contagious force of nature. No man can walk among it all and emerge unenriched or unscathed. On the Shetland moors, with the sun on your face and salt on the wind, and further islands for your horizons, the brew can leave you reeling with its intoxications. I love it all as much as I crave it. As the lochs shine and the pipits shrill, the larksong pours on and on and on, the curlews yabber and croon, the snipe tick-tock away their first days of spring, the red-throats preen and bathe, flipping over and re-streamlining themselves, you may pause on a mile of track in North Yell and agree that for these 24 hours at least and on this fragment of the planet, your God, or whatever you hold to, has got it right.

I contemplate the two miles of track which still lie ahead of me as I retrace my steps. I can see almost all the route, and that exhilarates me. I have suddenly projected myself high above my own formal human presence, and as

Neil Gunn once put it, 'I came upon myself sitting there'. I revelled in the idea of my smallness inching its way across the moorland miles, of how good it feels to be briefly a fragment of landscape where the air is good and the elements wild. The 'being' of that hour and the barely controllable joy of just walking through it, a step at a time, imbibing its wildness - these are treasures you cannot buy. I walked through the late afternoon, and as I walked, I searched in my mind for a corollary between me just walking and the diver just swimming. I am not sure that I found it, but in that mood, two miles skipped by and I reached the car wishing there were still ten more.

Two days later that schizophrenic spring lurched back into the jaws of winter. A frenzy of storm shut the moors from sight, flung snows and hard rains on icy winds into the gaping embrace on every west-facing voe, tormented the high ground with sizzling salvoes of sleet. At the height of it I had to drive a few miles of east coast Yell, a tentative aquatic journey. As I returned I glimpsed through a hole in the storm a single whooper swan on a moorland loch a quarter of a mile from the road. Because it was too late for most whooper swans, because the bird looked from a distance as if it might be injured, and because I care more for whooper swans than most things, I put on every shred of wind and waterproofing I owned and squelched over the moor on a hasty compass bearing. When I reached the loch, the swan was neither injured nor distressed, merely late and alone, leaning as it swam into the tug of the wind, upending to feed, rising on its tail to flex and shake archangel wings, subsiding whitely down, an ensnared oasis of tranquillity in all that ferment of storm. The great skeins of wintering whoopers were long gone, quartered in the breeding grounds of Iceland. This bird's dilemma now was whether to follow or while away a bachelor's empty months until the tribes trumpeted the return of autumn.

> Leaned uncompliant
> on the wind, stung
> by the sleety weals
> of its whips. May
>
> - termagant witch! -
> eggs on the tribe,
> 'North! North!' with
> gasping misplaced winter.
>
> Shetland's watersheets
> are shorn of all swans

save this dishevelled
lone lingerer (too much

like me for comfort:
I too have overstayed
adrift and uncomplying
on shores like these).

Dare you shrug, swan,
at nature's bidding
knowing swans depend
on being bidden and complying,

dutifully feathering
the tribal nest? Will you
still stir, swan, late
and languorous, forsaking

smoored Shetland
for the trysting fires,
or chastely stay
and marry my summer?

AFTER THE MOORS, the valleys. Shetland's hills can enclose you, but never for long, never with any sense of claustrophobia. Always the valleys are open-ended, always the sea at one end. Always the winds flood or feather through, and every little hilltop has more of a sea view than a land view. As you wander through these lightly peopled places, you cut open slices of island life. Peat is carved and stacked in every corner of the land, and although the style of the cutting and the stacking varies, and the cutter is as likely to ride out to his workings on a motor bike as he is to walk there (and he probably walks only to and from his parked car), he still moves to an ageless rhythm. I watched one man cut peats like flat roof tiles, wearing a Rangers blue anorak, and saw his peats gathered at the roadside in Union Jack plastic carrier bags. It is difficult to imagine anything Union Jackish about Shetland; rather their flourishing of their own white and blue flag recalls the Swiss, where even in the high Alpine valleys, every other home flies its own flag, proclaims the land's individuality. Shetland is such a place, its own place, the colours of its individuality nailed to its mast.

The best of the valley lands lie north of Tingwall, where the land transforms abruptly. You have just driven past sheltering guillemots at the head of Weisdale Voe, and now the land greens and deceives. Farms - not crofts - crop up. Even trees prosper, though prosperity for any Shetland tree is relative. Fat-budded spring usually means June, and the winds tend not to wait for autumn to flay away the leaves. Kergord's plantations in Weisdale are so renowned that they are listed on the official tourist map, but their only distinction is that they are trees in Shetland. Sherwood Forest it is not. Still, the woodland floor has a fitted wall-to-wall carpet of lesser celandine yellow, so startling that you wonder how that flower sought out and found the only fragment of suitable habitat in hundreds of hostile square miles.

Weisdale is green and wide and douce enough to be the Scottish Borders, and an old textile mill building heightens the illusion, except that it is no Tweed or Yarrow which flows through the fields but a struggling burn you can often step across. Shetland is no more fluent with rivers than it is with trees and this softening of the landscape was no more effective than anywhere else in Shetland in sustaining its old populations. All along the high flanks of the hills are more ruins of cottages and steadings. You note that even here, where there is a measure of shelter at least, the Shetlanders built on the high windswept places. There is no attempt to hide a house away, because mostly there is nowhere to hide, so build four square to the winds, taking them all on the chin, deflecting nothing. Winds are a fundamental part of the experience of life in Shetland, and hiding from them is as false as it is futile.

Beyond Kergord, a track and the dwindling burn beckon north into the Valley of Kergord. Here is the most complete and hill-girt of all Shetland's valleys, the hills closing in beyond Upper Kergord, and briefly shutting out that sea-smitten land which lies beyond in any compass-point you care to name. You can cling to the valley's illusions for as long as you hold to the watercourse, but climb to the high ground of West Kame and the prospect west and north-west instantly floods with the waters of St. Magnus Bay and the bewilderment of voes which dive inland from Swarbacks Head.

It is a good place to pause, this high ground of the Valley of Kergord, for it is at the very heart of all Shetland, and reveals its every shade. First it unmasks the valleys' deception, showing up the flimsy toehold by which they cling to the greater Shetland landscape, and that for all the assured calm of the valleys from within, their walls are paper-thin hills, no more than a thrust of the moors which are all Shetland's preference in the land within.

The land which spills west from here and which the maps call Aithsting and Sandsting (and the Shetlanders call Westside) is sea-riven much of the way to Sandness and Papa Stour, but for a few brief miles west of Brig of Waas, the road burrows back among the hills and moors through a valley of a kind, and passes the wide mouth of another valley. It is that second valley which coughs up souvenirs of Shetland's lost civilisations, the valley called Scord of Brouster. Scord, according to John Stewart, is 'a valley crossing a ridge', which fits well enough here, and Brouster is from bru, a bridge, presumably the nearby Brig of Waas. Little is left of what was, a few discernible stone patterns in the hill grasses where once stood a large thatched house with a central hearth, outbuildings, stock enclosures, a single standing stone where the scord crosses its ridge. It is a neolithic scattering, 3000-1500 BC, and clear enough evidence has been gleaned of farming people, stone-tipped tools like hoes and ploughs (the stone survives, the wood of their shafts does not). They were deer hunters and they hunted amid birch and willow and hazel, they grew barley, and they lived in a fertile, populated valley. You walk its monumental sadness now, sheep-scoured and empty, and you mourn, for there is no reason to think the Scord of Brouster was unique, no reason to presume the emptiness of the land within was ever thus.

I wandered on to Sandness where a lochan with two whooper swans stopped me in my tracks. I asked a farmer for permission to cross his land to the loch and was accorded affable approval. We leaned on his gate and jawed about the ways of swans and Shetlanders and he spoke of his arrival at Sandness 20 years ago as if he had emigrated there from half a world away, instead of from Skeld, which is perhaps 15 miles away, ten as the solan flies. His farm stops at the shore, the fate of almost all Shetland's valleys (this one Trona Scord). So, I wandered his small bay at his recommendation, and gazed out at the fields of Papa Stour, the best in Shetland by his reckoning. I also disturbed a pair of eiders and persuaded them unwittingly into one more of those exquisite wildlife cameos which I seemed to encounter all over Shetland, and which linger still, vivid imprints on my memory. The ducks were stepping placidly from their water when we saw each other. My response was to freeze, theirs to step back through the first wave and lounge watchfully offshore. The water was that astounding turquoise shade of St. Ninian's Isle, and as its waves broke on the shore, the offshore wind snapped the tops off them and blew them back at the ducks as spray. So it was through that translucent screen of blown spray that I watched the eiders on their turquoise cushions of sea, and between waves they emerged unscreened. I watched it all and wondered what Tunnicliffe would have made of it.

So that is the land which spills west from West Kame above the valley of Kergord, and its themes vary only in degrees to the north and east and south. Wherever your roads lead you through the land within, you will see something

to stop your tracks, or lure you deeper into the land...a gull dropping a mussel on the road so that the shell cracks open, the road as a tool...a fish van with a musical box passes you on the coast road in Muckle Roe...a merlin locked on the tail of a frantic meadow pipit until the chase ends in a silent rain of small feathers...the ultimate irony of Shetland's old and new architecture, a model croft house complete with thatch, in the garden of a new bungalow at Bray...a rare heron stilting through the shallows of a lochan at North Roe.

Then there was that day I idled through the fog by the Loch of Ting, an eerie, sodden day with loch and the hills veiling and unveiling themselves in turn, the fog permitting hints of the sun then snuffing them within moments. Everything seemed to shift in that clammy cloak, but nothing moved. In that wheeling grayness I walked the drenched causeway down the spit of land which leads to the Law Ting Holm, the legislative epicentre of all Viking Shetland. I saw the gulls rise from the holm, saw them move across the mist like motifs on a printed curtain fabric, saw figures emerge darkly, heard strange-tongued voices, watched shadowy ceremony. I stopped and felt a prickling fear. I spoke and heard no sound of my own voice. The ceremony proceeded without interruption, without recognition of my presence. I tried the scrutiny of logic. Why would the gulls fly up at my approach if the holm was already full of people? Why could the figures neither see nor hear me although I could see and hear them? Why could I not hear myself? Why did I hear no gull clamour when the birds rose?

The mist shifted again against a buffet of wind. One more glint of sun won briefly through, striking an emerald clarity on the grass of the holm. The gulls screamed and there was neither sight nor sound of any human figures in the landscape. I shouted, and started at my own voice. More gulls rose, screaming. I walked back along the causeway, and the mist closed a new curtain at my back. The gulls slid down it and settled.

The Tings were local legal assemblies, the tools of Viking administration. At Shetland's Tingwall, at Tingwall in Rendall on Orkney, at Dingwall in Easter Ross, at Tinwald in Dumfries, at Tynwald in the Isle of Man, Norse Parliaments once reigned. Shetland's local divisions of Aithsting, Delting, Sandsting, Nesting, Lunnasting, are echoes of that regime. The Law Ting Holm at the Loch of Ting was the central Shetland Parliament and law court. The old causeway knew the step of their solemn procession. The walls of the valley knew the shouts of their debate. The drift of gulls cocked an ear at their powers of reasoning. The mist folded them away forever. There are secrets still, landlocked in the land within.

Chapter Five

THE LAND BEYOND

THE FOURTEEN westward miles between mainland Shetland and Foula amount to more than mere distance. Sheila Gear wrote in her captivating book, *Foula - Island West of the Sun*, that 'there will always be "us" and "them" - Foula and the rest of the world'. The rest of the world may be only a 15-minute flight away, give or take a headwind or a tailwind, give or take the sea fog, but it is a world of difference which awaits. Getting there is also different. I arrived half an hour early at Tingwall airport to be greeted with: 'Mr Crumley? Oh good. You're the only passenger so we'll be able to leave early.' The rest of the week was punctuated with jokes about my private plane.

So I flew west over a map of Shetland big enough to be able to count the ruined crofts, which were many, big enough to pick out the Gothic stacks of Westerwick, then the plane nosed into a bank of fog and the only view was down, then it parted and Foula emerged as a sawn-off mountain range. The plane banked and dropped towards a wide convex dirt track and a hut which Foula defines as the airport, and I touched down beyond the rest of the world.

If you like your hills well herded into a small space, bonxies as thick on the ground as pebbles on a shore, if you like your telephone box to say 'Press button A', next to no roads carrying next to no traffic, if you like no-pub-no-shop-no-cafe-no harbour seasides, sea breezes which ram their freshness down your throat with over-zealous gusto, if you like a quietly independent tribe of natives, above all if you like coasts which climb vertically to the hilltops, you may find Foula contains all you need in a world. For all that administrators anchored dimly in the rest of the world - in this case Lerwick - have never found it convenient to administer such a place as Foula (the inconvenience has largely been used as a convenience for particularly relaxed administrating), there is a new school, a new pier, and a new aerogenerator. Comparisons with St. Kilda are as irresistible to visitors as they are tiresome to locals, but the evidence of your own eyes is hardly symptomatic of impending evacuation. Sheila Gear put it this way:

'The St. Kildans were landlubbers with a close-knit co-operative society based on fowling, living side by side in a crowded little street - an extraordinary idea to anyone here, where the houses tend to be on the outer edges of the crofts as far apart as possible. In 1930 a total evacuation of St. Kilda took place - an event that will never occur here. Excessive dependence on one another is a bad thing and makes an island very vulnerable. So we stand on our own feet and go our own way. Our pride in our island might be mistaken for conceit. One may insult a true islander or even insult his family, but one should never insult his island! And if we are condescending we can be excused - isn't our island the best in the world and should we not pity all those poor folk who have to live elsewhere?'

She also wrote: 'Always our hills are changing, always our eyes are drawn to them, always we are refreshed by them.' They are, to be sure, an exquisite flock of shapes, and your eyes become not so much drawn to them as magnetised by them. They are hardly a mere backdrop to island life either, for they are two-thirds of the island. Besides, the sun's circumnavigation of the island in any season of the year plays tricks with their every shape and shade and emphasis and profile, beckoning and rebuffing you, throwing barriers of hill up where you swore there was a valley an hour ago, or opening sesames where you swore there were barriers. The compactness of the group achieves shifts of landscape and perspectives in yards which would take miles to achieve in wider terrains, the kind the rest of the world knows about. So although you can skip over all Foula's summits in two or three hours, you could pass a cheery enough life learning to love their company.

I cut my teeth climbing up from the road to Ouvrafandal Loch, a black-watered meadow-fringed watersheet which looks from above like a green Polo mint. It lies in the green lap of the hills, and as hill lochans go, it is perfect, especially if you are a bonxie. There were hundreds on the water, and at my skylining presence they rose thick as geese, but silent as moths. Foula has 3,000 breeding pairs which is a lot for an island three miles by two, and in the nesting season, a lot of hostility. Higher up the meadowy floor of what becomes a steep grassy corrie, the birds gather round a cluster of lochans the colour of ripe blaes. They bathe often and energetically in fresh water and choose the greenest ground to dry off and preen. The incongruous quacking chorale of so many birds shunts around the walls of the hills, their spring and summer anthem.

From the summit of Hamnafield the island reveals all the splits in its personality, highland, lowland, and - in the wide corridor of the Daal - neither one thing nor the other. The hills reel away north-west, a curving, arcing spine topped off with the Sneug at 1,371 feet. In the lowering late afternoon light the hillsides furrow down to the meadow of Ouvrafandal, gathering at the foot like feathers. But it is the western ocean where your eye lingers from the summit of the Sneug, drowning in its scope. This is where Foula really is, not 14 miles west of anything, but a small mountain top of the north ocean. I think it is for that reason that Foula rather got under my skin.

The island is not west of the sun, though, not from the Sneug in the late afternoon at least, for there is the sun, slipping seawards in the evening, the evening of the west. It is a good PR cliché of course, because it works on the basis that the proportion of the rest of the world which claps eyes on Foula thinks of it as rooted to the western skyline, and it may as well be west of the sun.

Beyond the Sneug, the hill dips then rises to the Kame, the kind of summit which catches in your throat, for with no hint or dire warning it rises, steepens, narrows, flattens, stops. You are now 1,000 feet above the ocean with a vertical rock wall beneath your feet, and nothing at all beneath them should you take two paces forward. This awesome corner of Foula, and the headiest shore in all Shetland, is sniffily dismissed by the islanders as 'Da Banks', but misrepresentation is a good trick on Foula. The short inlet by the pier is 'Da Voe', but it is about as much voe as the Sneug is Matterhorn. It's all a question of scale, and a voe is a voe when it's the only one you've got. When you have more cliffs than you know what to do with, why play them up? Besides a voe is more crucial to the wellbeing of the Foula folk than a 1,000-foot wall.

But it is quite a wall, and it begins to unveil itself as you pause on your way down Soberlie, which is the hill's name rather than a commentary on the descent. The sun bore down out of the north-west illuminating a throng of verticals, and striking up bands of yellow and green and gray in the cliff face like prison bars. A small haze lifts from the sea, a frail film, enough to diffuse the light and tint the air, but not enough to blur shapes and outlines. Da Banks plunged and soared, seaward and skyward in the same motionless moment - sometimes the eyes suggested up, sometimes down, sometimes a fulmar flight would drag your eye across the cliffs, but there were no horizontals to focus on here, and if you chose to follow the bird, the eyes wallowed in the way that you stumble across the furrows of a newly-ploughed field.

But after a short spell of this showy coast's bombardment of your sensibilities, you find yourself coasting. Eyes drift, and your mind yields to nature's onslaught, quite overwhelmed and far beyond the point of sustained concentration. You might turn your back on the shore at that to be refreshed, in Sheila Gear's phrase, by the hills, and find them shorn of their moorit fleece and burning gold in evening's gladrags. The angling light illuminates too the shelf-like nature of the lower hills, a disarray of tilting planes patterned with the same furrow-feathers you saw from the Sneug, and capered by a rough-and-tumble of Shetland ponies giddy with the light.

The coast plunges on down to its lowest ebb, from where the Kame rears over your shoulder to full height, a guardsman among cliffs. The nearer cliffs have been massively gouged hundreds of feet above the sea where the heart has fallen out of the rock walls to lie unbeating in shattered masses at the tide's edge. One such bouldery shambles has been colonised by guillemots and their bibs glowed white-gold in that hypnotic light. Puffins whirr about the airspace now, in and out of the cliffs overhung midst, in and out of the tunnelled banks where you stand. Again the kittiwakes are holed up in a darkly reverberating corner of the shore, beneath a vast natural arch, where their cries ricochet and the echoes chase each other from wall to wall and back. The sound and the spectacle of them turned my mind back to their unchallengeable vulnerability in the sand eel controversy; this would be a miserable corner without the drama of their pageantry, but it may yet come to that.

Beyond the arch, the north coast of Foula has gathered a connoisseur's show of stacks and skerries, of which the star is Gaada Stack, now grown dramatically and imposingly since you first caught its unblinking eye from the summit of Hamnafield. With that memory-jogging moment in your mind, you turn to see Hamnafield from Gaada, and as you turn you are aware that after the sensations of the high cliffs, the sensations of the low ones (so puny from the Kame) do not suffer from the comparison. Foula's hills which looked mountainous from afar and Cuillin-pointed from the plane now heave mightily from beneath. This is the wizardry of Foula. Its landscapes consistently slip in and out of gear, consistently revise the judgements you have made, then revise the revisions. Always the landscape you thought you had pinned down regroups while you turn your head, so that when you turn again, you must pin it down anew.

So to Gaada, the showstopper. When I arrived on Foula, Colin had already been prowling the island for several days, and by walking and watching and trial and error - there are no short cuts - he had set up Gaada Stack, calculating that given a 'red blob' sunset the sun would pose briefly at a certain time of the evening, and shine right through the stack's 'eye'. We gather, the Baxter tribe and I, in front of the stack just before the appointed hour, and the evening which melted before us was one of the most subtle splendour I have ever watched. It was over in perhaps 40 minutes, but in that time, as the sun dipped and reddened and hardened into a perfect blood-coloured symbol of itself (and as it slipped and posed perfectly as predicted, a flaming iris to the stack's eye) sea and rock and light performed a dream sequence of nature. As I recall it now, I remember the banter and the jokes that sparked off the rocks, I remember the mounting excitement as the sun performed precisely as required, so that I felt again that I should applaud, but mostly I remember one exchange of incredulous glances, photographer to writer and back, which spoke everything we could have said about what we were watching. Ah, you had to be there.

The Noup is the PS to Foula's hills, out on its own across the Daal, a quiet pause of a place surveying the crofts of Hametoon, the thrusting finger of Sooth Ness. It turns its back on the other hills and its two fronts to the sea, contrives a protective arm and shoulder for Hametoon to lean on. On its summit is a small stone, carved simply with the shape of a two-sailed boat and the initials BI and either BB or BR or RR, and the date May 14, 1807. I had already resolved to research its significance when I was struck by the powerful notion that instead I should mark only its symbolic presence. (That was not a cop-out, for I had already beavered to good effect in the Shetland Room of Lerwick's fine library and it would have been no hardship to return.) So I left its stone unturned, and in fingering its weathered carving I saw that the pattern and shading of lichens across the stone looked like nothing so much as a sailor's chart. It is a sea place, Foula, and there is no getting away from it.

THAT IMPOSSIBLY far island shape on the clearest of evenings on the Noup is Foula's landscape brother of Shetland's land beyond. It is the one they call Fair Isle. For me Fair Isle's tilting tabletop will always be less of a landscape and more of a people place than Foula, than much of Shetland for that matter. The islanders sailed close to the wind in the 1940s when the population had withered away, and evacuation was in the air. St. Kilda was still vivid in memories all over the western and northern islands of Britain. But the Fraser Darling-like vision of an ornithologist called George Waterston turned the tide away from that fate. He bought the island for £3,000 in 1948, established a bird observatory and six years later sold the island to the National Trust for Scotland, and a benevolent partnership of islanders, Trust and observatory has initiated and sustained a process of slow change for the better which progresses still. There is more isolation here than on Foula, and fewer saving graces of landscape. There are no hills for refreshment, and without such a bulwark against ocean weather, Fair Isle hosts winds which think nothing of tossing a breaking Atlantic wave clear across the island into the North Sea. If you are contemplating a move to Fair Isle, you are advised by the islanders to test yourself against it in winter first. And Fair Isle lives in the way Sheila Gear insisted that Foula never could, in a huddle at the bottom end of the island, and with twice as many people – around 70 – as Foula.

But any encounter with the islanders leaves you with the impression of a calm and committed tribe, the perfect democracy in which community decisions are taken by the Fair Isle Committee (membership is the right of every resident adult), and whose ambitions for their small society are enshrined in a management plan which was prepared with the Trust's assistance. There is, for example, a presumption against holiday cottages, and when the old north lighthouse was automated the islanders demolished the keepers' cottages rather than see them become holiday homes. If you live on Fair Isle you live on Fair Isle and you live for it.

Fair Isle's is a subtler lure. The coast is fine, punctuated with all the geos, gloups and things you could wish for, but its cliffs are hardly Foula, or Westerwick or Eshaness. Sheep Rock is the cocked-hat landscape symbol of the island, but when you translate it from the guidebook photographs to reality, it is its smallness which surprises, that and the fact that it is a chancy place in a gale to go shepherding. Ward Hill in the north-west of the island, which at 712 feet is as high as Fair Isle gets, unfurls all the landscape the island has to offer. If you are blessed with a glittering clarity on the sea you might see Orkney and Sumburgh and Foula. Most likely you will see nothing but Foula and you will find it hard to stand up.

But there is an appealing terseness about the island, a kindly honesty which somehow pervades the land as it pervades the people. Nothing is hidden. What you see is what you get. I could live on Foula. I'm not sure I would have the bottle for Fair Isle.

There are always the birds, of course, and in such numbers and with such a consistent record in luring rarities that it also attracts spring and autumn migrations of birdwatchers. Most birdwatchers in my experience are thoughtful people whose interest ranges beyond birds, and often encompasses a broad-based understanding of all nature and a sensitivity to landscape and land use, and the people who use it. But there are those who harbour none of these qualities, whose passion is one-upmanship in rarities; they are hunters without guns, and their tick on the species list is little better than a stuffed bird in a glass case or a horned trophy on a shooting lodge wall. It says much for the tolerance of the Fair Isle folk that they thole such invasions more or less uncomplainingly. The problem is that Fair Isle being where it is, it is the perfect refuge for birds from North America or Asia whose migrations have gone wrong, and coughs up days which twitchers fantasise about. One such occasion, as recorded in Valerie Thom's thoughtful and thorough history, *Fair Isle – an Island Saga*, occurred on October 1 and 2, 1987. In the history books of twitching, it is enshrined like Bannockburn or Culloden. 'The migration log for these dates included Richard's and olive-backed pipits (W Siberia/NE Russia), rustic and little buntings (NE Europe), Radde's and yellow-browed warblers (Central Asia/ Siberia), red-breasted flycatcher (E Europe) and Scotland's first savannah sparrow from America.' If you were a twitcher and arrived on the 3rd of October, you probably climbed to the top of Ward Hill and threw yourself off.

A former warden at the Bird Observatory once told me that the saddest sight on Fair Isle is a group of twitchers who have just taken off from the island at the end of their stay, and as they look down at the island, they see a group of fellow-twitchers all running in the same direction, 'and' he added mischievously, 'they have no idea what the others have just seen. It's so sad'. And the grin tells you he was no twitcher.

The birds don't often seem to mind, however, for they still turn up in their exotic ones and twos, or in their humdrum thousands. That's what it is about Fair Isle - it's unquestioningly hospitable. Doesn't the whole place lie on the ocean like an open palm?

Chapter Six

THE DISTANT LAND

LERWICK, Saturday night, feverless. A thin rain wraps the gray toon like cellophane, it glistens and crinkles. I walk out into its calm wrap, staving off its chill with my left hand cupped round the fragrant furnace of a fish supper, my right dipping greasily into the hoard. Good fish suppers should be bought where they catch fish, eaten on the hoof in a harbour, inexpertly casting a land-lubber's blind eye on the ships and boats and battered in-betweens of every shade of grace and disgrace known to floating man.

The *Freedom*, the *Snowdrop* and the *Loki* have drowsed fender-to-fender for a week now, as far as I know. The first two are small fishing boats, the third a loveable mongrel suggesting a boat-builder who planned both a trawler and a houseboat and having run out of money or patience or both, cobbled them together, the hull of one, the superstructure of the other. She would be well cast in a remake of *The African Queen*. She shares with the others a painted stripe along her hull which ends with a flourish of two arrowheads at the bow, each urging the voyage forward. Perhaps next week.

Across the harbour lies the *Winsome*, from distant Scalloway - distant that is if you have to sail round Burra and Sumburgh Head, although a gull could drift from here to there on a favourable wind in about ten minutes. 50 yards of heaped nets lie on the quay beside her, but she shows little appetite for work, little inclination to live up to her name either. She's worked hard for her living though, and bears the scars. A pair of eider ducks cruise alongside, more winsome by far.

Some of the harbour's visitors throw deeper shadows. The *Azu* from Lagos has also been in an idle week, a careworn species of world traveller bruised by all the world's knuckle-dustered quaysides. The *Westra* from Leith, on the other hand, looks trig and trim but over-painted like a woman trying to hide her age behind too much make-up, an unflattering eggshell shade. These, and dozens more in the new, less appealing harbour to the north, are the flotsam and jetsam which the tides of half the world throw up on Shetland waters. Some never leave Shetland waters. Some will never be back. Some, like the *St. Clair*, wear a groove down the sea to and from Shetland, rubbing shoulders with Fair Isle with every trip, regular as tides. She sits there now in the dusk, her blue and black funnel perched high above the quayside, as much a part of the town's profile as the clocktower and the gray hill and its darkly burrowing closes.

On every Shetland shore tonight, boats are berthed or hauled high on noosts; off a few shores, ships are gratefully moored, small pauses, apostrophes on the page of the world's seas. Through all this moping inactivity, the Bressay ferry is breathlessly industrious, a restless spirit with two speeds - a fast scuttle

and stop. The rain, the ferry and the seabirds are the only moving parts of Lerwick's seafront tonight. The nervous herring gulls are suddenly bold as pigeons when I toss down a last scrap of fish. A black-back is suddenly in their midst, big as a cat, scattering allcomers, but it defers to a bonxie which gatecrashes the fray and wades in with the most fearless swagger in town. I have diced with them on Foula and St. Kilda where they are wild, elemental, aloof, handsome, spiritual almost. This scavenging down-and-out is an undignified traitor to his tribe. I turn my back on him and retire to spend my last night in Shetland - for the moment - in a room with a window which opens onto the Sound. As I go, I pass the *Bard*, the pilot boat, alight, primed, eager, offering a street-wise passage through the Sound to those freighters and fly-by-nights and tomato-soupy oilrig ships to which Shetland is a blurred convenience. The Bressay ferry glows east across the Sound in the rainy mirk.

Through the open window, the sounds of midnight ebb and flow in a doze of sleep...the tide slaps the old stone walls of old stone Lerwick, maalies paddle the water, dunter drakes squabble with rivals and concubines, the muted throb of the *Bard* calls to heel an obedient tomato-soup ship before unleashing her to the perils of the night sea, and (unmuzzled still) the sleepwalking Bressay ferry cuts across their wake. I awake at eight, and it is the Bressay ferry which wakes me.

ALL SHETLAND retreated from the rail of the *St. Clair*. I tried to pin down a single encapsulation of all my Shetland days, and could only narrow it down to two. One was on the low hill in a gale with Colin, somewhere up near Eshaness. He was trying to photograph Muckle Ossa, a far flung sea stack, using the longest of his lenses. The light grew better and better as the wind blew harder and harder. When holding the camera became impossible and a tripod would have collapsed into St. Magnus Bay, he set the camera up on the hilltop cairn, and carefully buried it with rocks, leaving the viewfinder, the end of the lens, the shutter button and the self-timer clear. 'Have a look,' he invited and I squinted down through the boulders and found the viewfinder filled with a quite breathtaking work of art - it is not too high an accolade. 'That', he said, 'is me all over.' He calls it 'grabbing rectangles' as though it were that simple, but we were both looking at the same landscape in the same light, and he had seen a rectangle which I had not.

It grew colder and colder, the light dimmed, and Foula skulked on the skyline like a gray marquee. Then the Eshaness lighthouse began to flicker on and off, the moon emerged, the sun set blankly. Colin found a new rectangle in which the critical component was the lighthouse light, that glow which was as brief as a matchflame in a gale and no bigger. We were here to make a beautiful book about a wild landscape, and this is how you make it, on a hilltop in a gale an hour before dark, shivering from the drip on your nose to the cramp in your left leg. No-one said it should be easy.

The second image I could not shake off was the graveyard at Hametoon on Foula. It is a functional, unsentimental place where the lichen on gravestone and ruined church was the same vibrant yellow shade as the ungrazed, uncut carpet of flowers, a match so perfect no designer would have dared it. This is

something, to die, to 'moulder away and be like other loam' as Edwin Muir had it, and in death to nurture a flowering which so mirrors your small memorial. There is an elemental continuity about that undiscriminating spread of colour which seemed to bode well for an eternity of renewal. For now, Shetland is a distant land again and I miss it, but that eternity of renewal is what I ask for its landscape and all its tribes and fellow travellers.

As the *St. Clair* slipped past Sumburgh Head, I saw Foula emerge almost in the same instant as I laid to rest the memory of the Hametoon yellow. I watched the island until it was nothing, and – I swear it! – it was west of the sun.

SHETLAND

Land of the Ocean

THE LAND OF THE SWORD

The Land of the Sword is all Shetland. If you hold to the most popular theory
about the derivation of the word 'Shetland' - that it is from 'Hjaltland', 'hjalt' being the Norse for the
crosspiece of a sword, you will have little trouble fashioning a sword shape from the island map. The landscape
also fits the definition well, for it depends for its effect on its sea-cutting edges, the discreet
strength of its bladed rock, the brown scabbard of peat-deep hills. And through all
Shetland's turbulent history, there are surely no more sword-smitten
islands than these.

Spring snow, Strom Ness peninsula, the Clift Hills far to the south.

Headlands of West Burra and Oxna island, towards the south shores of Sandsting.

Bright and boisterous seas in a bay of Kettla Ness, West Burra.

Harry's Pund, one of a group of resoundingly named rocks near Hillswick, Northmaven.

Graveyard on the sea's edge, Ness of Trebister, Bressay beyond.

Lee of Saxa Vord, mighty flank of Burra Firth, North Unst.

THE LAND OF THE OUTER SHORE

The Land of the Outer Shore is the battleground of the oldest war in
the world, the ocean against the rock. Always the rock loses. There were mountains
here once. Now there are jagged headstones to mark their passing. Here is the sea's cutting edge at
work and its smashing edge, and its battering ram. Here the rock succumbs to stacks, geos, gloups,
blowholes, caves, into a stuttering and shambolic beauty. Through it all, seabirds throw up
towering spring cities which they evacuate before winter seas wreak
the most desolate havocs of all.

Basalt lava cliffs and stacks, Brae Wick, Eshaness.

Kittiwakes relish huge seas near Eshaness lighthouse.

Noss and Bressay crowd the horizon above Greenmow, South-East Mainland.

Ocean-going cliffs of Muckle Roe in the heart of St. Magnus Bay.

Dore Holm, primeval holed stack off Eshaness, with passing cloud.

North Sea mists thicken the murky sounding Horns of Hagmark, North Unst.

Showy stars of the sea-bird cliffs – Puffin, Black Guillemot, Fulmar.

Spring sunlight soothes Foula's battered north coast.

Fractured cliffs of Hermaness, Unst – Shetland's northmost shore.

Stormy seas hurdle Moo Stack on the west shore of Eshaness.

Two northern outposts of Mainland Shetland – Uyea Island . . .

. . . Ramna Stacks beyond the headland of Fethaland.

THE LAND OF THE INNER SHORE

The Land of the Inner Shore is the Shetland of sheltered
sounds and of the voes, sea lochs which eat deep into the land, so deep at times that the
land is almost bisected into new islands. Sometimes an island sits in the mouth of the voe with the turbulent
ocean on the one side, the placid voe on the other. Here, after the melting of the ice sheet, the sea
rose too quickly, drowned river valleys, fashioned islands from hills. Here the sea lies, trapped
by its own avarice. Here too lies one of Shetland's best theatres for
the play of light and water and landscape.

Causeway, Bridge of Walls, West Mainland, and the headland of Browland.

Nature's causeway – showpiece tombolo linking St Ninian's Isle to Mainland Shetland.

Cribba Sound threads the mazy landscape of Vementry, Papa Stour on the horizon.

Characteristic two-prowed boats at Sandwick, South Mainland.

Voescapes - the heart of Whiteness Voe, Nesbister Point on left . . .

. . . pier at Skeo Head deep in the elbow of Ronas Voe.

Weisdale Voe beyond the peninsula ridges of Whiteness and Stromness . . .

. . . Weisdale Voe transformed by a fall of spring snow.

THE LAND WITHIN

The Land Within is that Shetland which the sea spares.
It is a small and spasmodic landscape of short valleys, brief rivers and high
lochan-strewn moors where handsome red-throated divers wail at the sky. The moors give rise to
low hills and the mainland traveller from far Scotland can be briefly deceived. But climb even the lowest
of the high ground and find sea on all four sides, see a ship pass the end of a river valley or the blink
of a lighthouse beyond a peat hag. Even in the deepest, widest moor,
the sea reaches you on a salty wind.

Startling summer green on a croft at Bixter Voe, West Mainland.

Traditional croft house, west coast of Yell – with discreet phone box.

A clutch of crofts, Braehoulland, North Mainland, and one of Shetland's many Hamna Voes.

Lone cottage, Fetlar and the coast of Yell beyond Colgrave Sound.

Post Offices at Heylor (left), Britain's most northerly at Haroldswick on Unst (top right), and Walls (bottom right).

Rich mix of land use at Flett, near Voe.

Snow-and-slate-gray landscape, The Firth and Sandsound Voe, West Mainland.

Shapely summit on Papa Little across The Rona.

Domed Ronas Hill, summit of all Shetland, dominates the North Mainland.

Well-worked crofting lands clustered round Burra Voe at North Roe.

THE LAND BEYOND

The Land Beyond is a fragmentary land. Even within as isolated
an archipelago as Shetland there are degrees of isolation, places like Out Skerries or
Fair Isle or Foula where even many Shetlanders never set foot. But unlike so many isolated
islands, the Land Beyond is a place of vigorous community life where the rest of the world drops
in by boat and plane but rarely lingers. The islands of the Land Beyond are small places but
their landscapes are vast, meagre rocks in immensities of sea and sky
and space, the widest horizons in all Shetland.

Foula - Shetland's 'island west of the sun' hugs the western horizon.

BUSINESS REPLY SERVICE
Licence NoIV1008

2

Colin Baxter Photography Ltd
PO Box 1
Nethy Bridge
Inverness-shire
PH25 3BR

If you would like to know more about Colin Baxter Photography publications and to receive regular information on new titles, please return this prepaid card.

Name ....

Address ....

....

.... Postcode ....

We are also pleased to receive any of your comments or suggestions regarding our publications.

....

....

....

Thank you

Westmost Foula - jutting cliffs at Wester Hoevdi (left) and Nebbifield (right).

The Noup, southmost of Foula's hills, across the flattened span of the Daal . . .

. . . and classically profiled across Hellabrick's Wick.

The Kame, fitting distant finale to Foula's North Bank (left), and in startling close-up (right).

Ouvrafandal from The Sneug, summit of Foula; sea mist rolls in on Hamnafield.

Fragments of Out Skerries – Lamba Stack (left); south-west outliers with Noss beyond (top right); east across South Mouth (bottom right).

Out-on-a-limb Out Skerries seen across Burravoe, South Yell.

Ler Ness, dominant in the view south from Ward Hill – Fair Isle's highest point.

South-west Fair Isle – Lang Cole prominent among the stacks north of Malcolm's Head.

Summer evening light silhouettes Stacks of Skroo off Fair Isle's northern cliffs.

North Lighthouse, guardian of Fair Isle's north-east corner.

Papa Stour – West coast Geo with far flung Foula (top left); old stone (bottom left); Stacks in Housa Voe (right).

Low sun pins breaking waves to Papa Stour's south-west cliffs.

Solitary unnamed stack off Stourhund, West coast of Papa Stour . . .

. . . and another nearby off Lyra Skerry and Fogla Skerry.

THE DISTANT LAND

The Distant Land is the Shetland of memory, the Shetland of
the compulsive island traveller who, having tasted Shetland, is restless for return.
It is the Shetland of seafarers and of headland-thudding seas, of razor-edge winds and
razor-sharp light. It is the Shetland of rock in every shape and shade and on every scale
from stacks and skerries, cliffs and headlands to horizon-clinging islands. It is the
Shetland of pungent moorland scents and long, burrowing voes, the clowning
of puffins and a single tern skidding above the tide.

Rockscapes – Noup of Noss (left), famed bird cliff, and the charismatic Drongs (right).

Finely prowed stack in Coppa Wick near Sandness – Papa Stour beyond.

Secret Shetland where memory lingers – Muckle Ossa far beyond Eshaness . . .

. . . and the quiet curve of a hidden beach on Ronas Hill's blind side.

Berry R. J. & J. L. Johnson	*The Natural History of Shetland*, Collins.
Brown, George Mackay	*Selected Poems*, The Hogarth Press.
Cruden, Stewart	*The Scottish Castle*, Spurbooks.
Cusa, Noel	*Tunnicliffe's Birdlife*, Clive Holloway.
Dey, J.	*Out Skerries – An Island Community*, Shetland Times.
Finnie, Mike	*Shetland – an Illustrated Architectural Guide*, RIAS/Mainstream.
Gear, Sheila	*Foula, Island West of the Sun*, Gollancz.
HMSO	*St. Ninian's Isle Treasure*, HMSO.
HMSO	*The Brochs of Mousa and Clickhimin*, HMSO.
Linklater, E.	*Orkney & Shetland*, Hale.
Malcolm, D.	*Shetland's Wild Flowers*, Shetland Times.
Marwick, E.	*Folklore of Orkney and Shetland*, Batsford.
NTS	*Fair Isle*, National Trust Scotland.
Nicolson, J. R.	*Traditional Life in Shetland*, Hale.
Ritchie, J. N. G.	*Brochs of Scotland*, Shire Archaeology.
Ritchie, A.	*Exploring Scotland's Heritage – Orkney and Shetland*, HMSO.
Schei, Liv Kjørsvik & Moberg, Gunnie	*The Shetland Story*, Batsford.
Scott, W. & Palmer, R.	*Flowering Plants of the Shetland Isles*, Shetland Times.
Stewart, John	*Shetland Place Names*, Shetland Times.
Thom, Valerie	*Fair Isle, An Island Saga*, John Donald.
Tulloch, B.	*Bobby Tulloch's Shetland*, MacMillan.
Tulloch, B.	*Migrations, Travels of a Naturalist*, Kyle Cathie.
Tunnicliffe, C. F.	*Bird Portraiture*, MacMillan.
Williamson, Henry	*Salar the Salmon*, Faber.

Colin Baxter's photographs of Scotland's landscape and cities appear in over twenty books, a wide range of calendars and an ever-growing catalogue of postcards. His work also encompasses other areas of Britain, including the Lake District and the cities of Bath and York, as well as the landscapes of other countries, such as France and Iceland. He lives in the Highlands of Scotland.

Jim Crumley's poetic books about nature and landscape in Scotland include *A High and Lonely Place*, *Among Mountains*, *The Heart of Skye* and *Gulfs of Blue Air*. His work with swans has produced *Waters of the Wild Swan* and *The Company of Swans* and has been featured on BBC TV and Radio 4. He is also the author of the personal 'homage' to Dundee, *The Road and the Miles*.